ACTION THIS DAY

Action this Day

LETTERS FROM
THE FIGHTING FRONTS

BY

FRANCIS J. SPELLMAN

Archbishop of New York
Military Vicar of the Armed Forces
of the United States

NEW YORK
CHARLES SCRIBNER'S SONS
1943

TO THE CHAPLAINS

AMERICA, REBORN

Lord, lift this mighty host that is America;
Reconsecrate us in devotion to Thee.
Too oft have we forgot our heritage of faith—
The mess of pottage to our eyes was dear,
The gold within our coffers deadened us:
We, who by nature are between the earth and sky,
Earthward have sunk, and drunk of miraged visions.

But now, reborn,
We lift again to Thee our nation's soul.
Behold, we are Thy wheat,
Nurtured beneath the sunshine of the plains;
We are Thy grapes from vineyards in the sun,
And timber from Thy forests;
Ours are the iron sinews torn from earth's deep breast,
And oil from her rich arteries.

O God, we build anew and dedicate again to Thee
The host and temple of America—
Many we are, in space wide worlds apart,
But we are one today,
Made one by this, our common will:
That righteousness again shall walk among the sons of men.
Now, welded of our pain,
We would again be what our forebears were,

Men who did worship Thee,
And, mindful of Thy Fatherhood,
Could reach to brothers o'er the sea a brother's hand.
In every man we found Thy image then,
And, finding, wrote our nation's creed,
A pledge that made us the Samaritan
To the oppressed and lowly of the earth.
In those far days, our soul was young and clear,
We opened arms to all who suffered wrong;
We bowed not, in our youth, however strong the foe,
For we were strong in loyalty to Thee,
And strong in faith that all men should know freedom
And worship Thee in freedom, as conscience should direct.

And now,
Amidst the ruins of a world that strove
To prosper and to live apart from what was bought,
On Calvary, by Christ, Thy Son—
Now we come back by that well-trodden way
That prodigals of every age have walked,
Back to our higher destiny—to Thee,
Our Father and our God,
And, kneeling in the valley of our grief,
Rededicate (both we who here must work
And those, our sons and brothers overseas,
Who still perhaps must die),
Rededicate ourselves to the great task that still remains,
That on the altar of our common victory,
Not to a god of war,
But to the Lord of Peace,
We give ourselves anew within the wounds

Of Him in Whom all men are one—
For all may yet redeem their faulty past,
Held in these wounded Hands of Christ, our Great High Priest.

We are a single host of grateful love for Thee,
A single will for universal peace for men,
A single soul of righteousness to come!
Lord, lift this mighty host that is America,
Reconsecrate us now in Thy Son's Holy Name.
                    Amen.

+Francis J. Spellman

INTRODUCTION

I had no idea of writing about the six months' trip which I have just concluded. On the contrary, for several reasons, I had the idea not to write about it. I have made many journeys, visited many places, had many experiences, and I have never written about any of them. Naturally, I expected from time to time either publicly or informally to relate various happenings and make reference to them in ways that might help the cause in which I am interested: the spiritual and temporal welfare of my fellow-man.

It has now been represented that what I have written might be of interest to those who have dear ones serving with our armed forces, to whom, also, I am devoted, and whom I am desirous to serve.

It is impossible for me to write all that occurred, all that I saw, all that I heard, all that I did. I met persons about whom many-volumed biographies can and will be written. I visited countries whose histories, fluctuating geographies and complexities fill library shelves. I witnessed scenes, learned of situations, and participated in happenings about which the world has been informed by official statements, by daily reportings from thousands of competent observers, capable writers, outstanding photographers.

I have no intention of attempting biographies, writing miniature histories or appraising military or political situations.

I traveled alone; I was occupied every day from early morning until late at night and occasionally through the night. But, following a custom, begun in boyhood when I was away from home, I did write letters.

Through the four years at Fordham College, New York, and five years at North American College, Rome, I wrote each week to my mother. Likewise did I write to her during the seven years that I was attached to the Vatican Secretariate of State. During this period I visited every European country from the Baltics to the Balkans.

After my mother's death, I continued the same custom, writing to my father when I was away from home, for example, in 1938, giving him accounts of my visits to all the countries of South America. Within the past year I have written to him from various parts of our own country, from Canada, Alaska, and the Aleutian Islands. I followed the same practice during this recent trip.

These letters in simple narrative form tell something of the places I visited, something about the people I met, and some incidents which one would naturally include in writing letters home. They resemble in matter and form the letters that at the present time hundreds of thousands of men and women are writing home. This book, therefore, professes to be nothing more than a series of letters, for the most part just as they were originally written without any effort to be erudite or comprehensive.

Obviously, I am not writing all my thoughts or recounting all that occurred or describing all that I saw. Cardinal Gasparri told me that when he was asked to write his memoirs he declined, saying: "The interesting things I cannot tell, and the things which I can tell are not interesting." I have respected all confidences and yet I am told that what I have written is interesting. Therefore, I have given these letters to the Military Ordinariate with the request that the proceeds be used in their entirety for the welfare of the soldiers and sailors of all races and religions who visit the Cathedral Canteen in New York City. This organization provides luncheons and dinners without cost to all servicemen. Thousands of them, from every branch of the service, from all parts of the country and overseas, visit this canteen each week. All are heartily welcomed as friends and neighbors.

The title, "Action This Day," was suggested by a little card which Winston Churchill took from his desk and gave to me. Mr. Churchill has a variety of such cards for the disposition of various matters. "Action This Day" is not only a good title but a good maxim for every one every day.

FRANCIS J. SPELLMAN

My dear father:

On Thursday morning, February 4th, I had the honor of an
audience with President Roosevelt. On previous occasions, I
had already discussed with the President the desirability of
making a trip to see the Chaplains in the overseas war zones. I
had completed the visitation to a great number of Chaplains
in this country, in Canada, Alaska, and the Aleutians, and I
thought it might be opportune to visit others in their overseas
posts. The President had indicated that I might start my journey some time during the first week in February subsequent to
his own return from Casablanca.

The President looked very well and was, as always, extremely
cordial, frank, encyclopedic in his knowledge, and contagiously
optimistic. He told me some of the experiences of his trip. The
President does not enjoy traveling by air. Besides physical dis-
comfort, or rather on account of it, he is unable to do much
work or read or talk. In such circumstances flying above the
clouds for hours becomes very monotonous. For my own part,
I enjoy flying whether I read, talk or just look out the window
and think.

I told the President that everything was in readiness for my
journey and that my passport with the visas from Portugal to
China was already in my pocket. I told him, too, that I had
had all my inoculations, that I had been vaccinated against
cholera, smallpox, typhus, yellow fever, typhoid, paratyphoid,

and tetanus, and that I planned to leave on Tuesday, February 9th.

I thanked the President for his kindness, and I also expressed appreciation for the help I had received from the Secretary of State, Mr. Cordell Hull, the Under-secretaries of War and Navy, Judge Robert F. Patterson and Honorable James V. Forrestal, Colonel Roy Ireland of the Air Transport Command, and Mrs. Ruth Shipley of the State Department.

With an assurance of continued prayer that God would bless his efforts to lead our country on the road to victory, peace, and prosperity, I took my leave. As I left the office, I met Admiral King, the Commander-in-Chief of our Navy, and General Holcomb, the Commandant of the Marine Corps. They were accompanying General Vandergrift, who was to receive from the President the Congressional Medal of Honor.

There had been a suggestion that I be accompanied on the trip, but, for several reasons, I declined. I deeply appreciated the thoughtful courtesy of the proposal, but since I had been accustomed to assist other people in their travels, I felt that I would not need assistance in my own. I would also have felt embarrassed and disturbed if any one who could have been doing something else had been assigned to look after me, for I have always taken care of myself, at least to my own satisfaction. Besides, I was well fortified with letters of introduction, and those to whom I was to present them could certainly care for me alone more easily than for two of us.

On Saturday, February 6th, I went to Boston to attend the regular monthly meeting of the Chaplains and the dinner given to the group being graduated that month from the Chaplains' School at Harvard University. These meetings are interesting and helpful, primarily because they afford an opportunity for the Chaplains and for us to become mutually acquainted.

I took advantage of this visit to Boston to see you and the other members of the family, to tell you that I planned to be away from home for some time, and to say good-bye. I did not tell you of my destination but I imagined you guessed that I hoped to go far. I went to Framingham to see my aunt in the convent. After a short but pleasant visit with Sister Philomena, I returned to New York on the midnight train.

On Sunday morning in the Cathedral, I celebrated the nine o'clock Mass for the members of the Newman Club Federation. After Mass I met Mr. and Mrs. Thomas Francis Sullivan, of Waterloo, Iowa, the parents of the five boys who were lost when the U. S. cruiser *Juneau* was sunk. They were happy and consoled to learn from me something that I had just heard, that although the *Juneau* did not have a priest on board at the time it was sunk, the ship had been visited only two days earlier by a Chaplain from another vessel. He had heard the confessions of the Catholic men aboard and given them Holy Communion at a Mass said just before the ship sailed to meet the enemy. Mr. and Mrs. Sullivan are certainly exemplary in their heroic, spiritual, Christian, American viewpoint.

Today, my last full day at home, I offered Mass for the Sullivan boys, in the presence of their father and mother before the shrine of Our Lady of New York in St. Patrick's Cathedral.

I packed two bags until I had fifty-five pounds. I delivered them to the Pan-American Airways office and paid for my ticket to Lisbon. I had prepared as well as I could for the trip that was before me. I had some concentrated foods, pills for the decontamination of water, and small cans of powdered milk. The instructions on the bottle containing the pills for purifying water were that one pill was to be put into a pint of water, but if the water was *very* polluted, two pills should be used! I disposed of all current matters and cleared my desk. I appointed the Vicar General, Right Reverend Monsignor Joseph P. Donahue, administrator of the Archdiocese of New York.

I am ready to go. I realize that of the many long journeys that I have made during my lifetime this one will be unique. Whatever the outcome, I feel certain that I shall be glad I undertook the trip. I bid "good-bye" to you and the family. I shall write you as often as possible.

God bless you!

Early in the morning of February 9th, Bishop O'Hara, Bishop McIntyre, and Monsignor Casey went with me to the airport. The English officials had put on every possible visa except the one that I needed first, the one for Bermuda. We telephoned to the British Consul and were told that there would be no difficulty about the matter as the Governor of Bermuda, Viscount Knollys, had been informed of my coming.

The formalities at the airport were very quickly attended to through the kindness of Major Bickley. The time passed pleasantly until the scheduled departure at 8.30. We were delayed somewhat because one of the passengers had not been sufficiently investigated by one of the government departments. Later we were again delayed because of a defective radio receiver.

I had already said good-bye and had boarded the plane, when we were notified of this second delay. We went ashore once more, and once more there were good-byes and good wishes. The ship was the ATLANTIC CLIPPER; its pilot was Captain Lewis, and his co-pilot was Captain Gallagher.

It was evident that I was not the only passenger that had been up all the night, for shortly after the ship left the water, many of the passengers went to sleep. Tired as I was, the man who had the place in the plane opposite me was even more tired, because he became slightly annoyed after the plane started, to be awakened, first of all in order to be relieved of his hat, and secondly, to be asked if he didn't wish a piece of gum! We had luncheon on the plane at one o'clock, and by that time nearly all the passengers were awake.

Even in wartime it is easy to make acquaintances on clipper airships. Several of the passengers I had met before. One of them, a Belgian Minister of State, had visited me only a few days previously to tell me of the dire poverty, the sufferings, and the starvation of the children of Belgium, and asked me if there were any way I could help to save them. It was not a question of financial assistance but rather of obtaining permission from the Allies to send food through the blockade for the Belgian children without indirectly helping Germany.

More than ten years had passed since I had crossed the ocean. As you remember, I had not been in Europe since 1932, when I was consecrated a Bishop. Several times I had wished to return to Europe for a visit and for a long time I had a reservation for the first commercial Trans-Atlantic passenger flight. I was prevented from making this trip, however, because at that very time, I was transferred from Boston to New York.

It was but a short flight to beautiful Bermuda, and the brilliant sun, sky, and sea, the bright green of the trees and grass offered a startling contrast to the dull winter New York day I had just left. We remained in Bermuda a few hours during which time I was the guest of the Governor, Viscount Knollys. From the landing stage of the clipper, we went in the Governor's barge to the dock at Hamilton, proceeding then in a two-horsed carriage from the quay to the Governor's home where I met Lady Knollys. Their home is beautiful, commodious, convenient, and a bit "antiquish."

Time passed quickly and pleasantly talking with Mr. Beck,

the American Consul, and with Admiral James of our Navy and soon I was back in the plane leaving Bermuda, and on my way to Horta in the Azores, where we were due the following morning. We had our evening meal, and since, on leaving Bermuda, we had only twenty-four of our original forty-two passengers, there was room for each of us to have a bunk. The clipper can seat seventy-four persons. Two stories were current regarding this plane: one to the effect that it carried President Roosevelt to Casablanca for his historic conferences with Winston Churchill; the other, that it was the escort plane of the President.

I went to bed about eleven o'clock and slept well, awakening in the morning at seven, just before our arrival in Horta. It was a long sleep for me. It was thrilling to fly over and look on the Azores, those islands in the mid-Atlantic, possessions of Portugal, from which many immigrants have come to America. We planed down to a smooth landing in the harbor. We were fortunate to have had calm water, as all too frequently the swell of the waves prevents landings and take-offs for considerable periods.

Immediately on arrival, I had a ride in an especially diminutive and especially old automobile which brought me to the Cathedral where I offered Mass. The Bishop was not on this island; no one asked me to identify myself and I did not volunteer identification. While I was at the Cathedral, the other passengers had breakfast. In the meanwhile, the beds in the airship were re-transformed into seats. The ship had been cleaned and refueled and was ready for departure. We left Horta about nine o'clock, and the flight to Lisbon was smooth. We arrived there about six o'clock in the evening. Viewed from the air, Lisbon is a picture. It stretches out for miles along the banks of the

Tagus River. Like Rome, it is a seven-hilled city. Arriving there just at sunset, I found it inexpressibly beautiful.

We landed on the Tagus River near Lisbon, and soon we were at the dock. Mr. Cootes and Mr. Nunn of the American Legation met me and accompanied to a hotel where a room had been engaged for me. The following morning, I met Mr. Bert Fish, the American Minister. He was most cordial. We talked of various things of current interest: the war; America's contribution to its successful prosecution; of places in the world with which we were both familiar, and of mutual friends. I told Mr. Fish that I would like to proceed to the Vatican as soon as possible and return later to Portugal.

I then called on the Apostolic Nuncio, who, as you know, is the representative of the Holy See, accredited as ambassador to a government. The status of a nuncio differs from that of an apostolic delegate who represents the Vatican with the clergy and people, but not officially with the government as an ambassador.

The Nuncio of Portugal is Archbishop Ciriaci. I have known him for thirty-two years. One of my first Roman professors he became Undersecretary in the Vatican Secretariate of State when I was stationed there. I met him later in Prague when he was Nuncio to Czechoslovakia. Residing with Archbishop Ciriaci was Monsignor Mozzoni, formerly assigned to the Apostolic Delegations in Ottawa and London. Monsignor Clarizio of the Vatican Secretariate of State, in Lisbon on courier service, was also at the Nunciature. I enjoyed my meetings with them all. I profited by their discussion of world events, for their knowledge of various situations was accurate and detailed.

Reaching Portugal after ten years' absence from Europe was a bit disconcerting because even in the atmosphere, one feels tension and uncertainty. This impression may be due to my imagination, for, before coming to Lisbon, I had read and heard of all the espionage centered there. Nearly every one I met in Lisbon seemed to be on guard against something. One person on whom I called, and whom I met in his own office, disconnected his telephone from the wall socket, even though the receiver was on the hook. He said that he thought it possible that spies might hear our conversation. He had nothing to tell me and I had nothing to tell him, but he was cautious from force of habit.

The population of Portugal is over seven million; that of Lisbon, its capital city, about eight hundred thousand. The country is prosperous, especially now because of world conditions and Portugal's position as a neutral nation. Lisbon, however, bears some resemblances to the cities of belligerent nations. For example, there are very few automobiles in circulation. Those that are operated are powered with gasogen generated from coke.

The Portuguese people and Government admire America and like Americans. Dr. Salazar, the Prime Minister, had the respect of every one that I met. His reputation for integrity of life and honesty of purpose is excellent; and no one can question his ability to inspire confidence.

The Patriarch of Lisbon is Cardinal Cerejeira. His great concern seems to be the welfare of the Seminary which he established. Churches and church activities in Portugal are managed by lay organizations called confraternities; and the clergy have less responsibility in the direction of affairs concerned with religion than have the clergy in America.

Well content with my visit to Portugal, short but concentrated, I left Lisbon for Madrid, on Lincoln's Birthday, February 12th. Because Portugal and Spain are neutral countries, the shades of commercial airplanes are not drawn in flight, the way they are in our own country during wartime. The trip from Lisbon to Madrid lulled me into meditation. The landscape is varied. Portuguese and Spanish towns dot the hills and the plains. Fertile fields, arid wastes, snow-capped mountains, olive groves, castles, houses, and huts drift by in the panorama. We followed the Tagus River for a good part of the journey, and in three hours we were over the capital city of Spain, Madrid.

I was astonished to see the American Ambassador, Dr. Carlton J. H. Hayes, at the airport. The Nuncio to Spain, Monsignor Cicognani, and his secretary, Monsignor Calleri, were also there. Dr. Hayes invited me to be the guest of Mrs. Hayes and himself at the American Embassy. I have known them for many years and the invitation was so very sincere and cordial that I accepted and enjoyed very much being with them. In my opinion, Dr. Hayes is a most able representative of our country. His character, his background as scholar and historian, his ability to meet and to appraise people, and his patience, all these admirably fit him for his post. Mrs. Hayes is an ideal ambassador's wife. She is kind, intelligent, thoughtful, and untiring.

The American Embassy is a very imposing and at the same time comfortable residence built about thirty or forty years ago by the Duke and Duchess of Montellano. The Duchess is a Mexican lady named Escandon. The Embassy is a three-storied house and serves both as the office of the Ambassador and as his residence. Every day since I left New York has been full, sunshiny in every way, and living so pleasantly in this beautiful home, brings added brightness.

On my arrival at the Embassy, the Ambassador and Mrs. Hayes, their son Carroll, who is about seventeen years of age, the Ambassador's secretary, Michael George, and myself had luncheon together. In the afternoon the Ambassador and I drove to the "University City" and saw the tremendous damage caused by the Civil War. We went as far as the Prado, where General-issimo Franco lives in a palace surrounded by a great park. It is amazing and depressing to see the damage wrought by the violence of battle in which fifty thousand people perished in the city of Madrid. Ruins that are centuries old have a certain beauty and charm about them but there is nothing pleasant about the gaunt specter of death and destruction that hovers over these ruins of great and modern buildings. These buildings, now de-molished, were the pride of Spain, the center of its intellectual and cultural life.

After this drive, the Ambassador and myself called on the Apostolic Nuncio, Monsignor Cicognani. From former visits to Madrid I well remember the Nuncio's residence. A tablet on the staircase commemorates the fact that Pope Benedict XV was a former Papal Nuncio to Spain.

Up three flights of stairs and down corridors extending the length of three sides of the palace, we came to the official apart-ment where His Excellency the Nuncio received us. Before meeting him at the airport on my arrival, I had seen Monsignor

Cicognani only once, namely, on the occasion of the consecration of Bishop William O'Brien in Chicago. At that time Monsignor Cicognani was passing through the United States, having been transferred from his post as Nuncio to Peru to become Nuncio to Vienna. He profited by the opportunity to visit his brother, the present Apostolic Delegate to the United States. During this visit to Madrid, we became well acquainted. He sent a telegram to the Vatican announcing that I had arrived in Madrid, and that I would proceed to Rome on the first available plane.

That night we had an early dinner at the American Embassy. It was at least an early dinner for Spain, for we sat down at table at eight o'clock, whereas the customary time is nine-thirty or ten o'clock. The reason for this unorthodox acceleration in eating time was that the Ambassador had arranged to have a showing of an American moving picture at a theater in the city. Members of the Government, the diplomatic corps, and other friends of the Ambassador were among the invited guests. There was a tremendous demand for the tickets and I felt sorry for the Ambassador because there were not enough seats for all who wished to go. But at least he could show the film another time, and Bishop O'Hara never could arrange to have the Army-Notre Dame football teams play more often than once a year to help him out of his annual ticket predicament! The Ambassador graciously invited me to attend this presentation of the film, but I preferred to remain at home so that, for a change, I could go to bed before two o'clock in the morning. Dr. Hayes said that he had been asked by some news agencies about me and whether I had anything to say to newsmen. I replied that I had nothing to say except that I had been invited to celebrate Mass in the

Madrid Cathedral on Sunday, that I intended to do so, and that in a few days I hoped to continue to the Vatican by way of Barcelona.

On Saturday, February 13th, I went with Father Molina, a Spanish Franciscan, to visit the famous Escorial Palace. Father Molina made his studies at St. Bonaventure College, Alleghany, New York, and at the Catholic University, Washington, D. C. He was also stationed for a time in New York City and greatly admires America. He is a pleasant, kindly, well-informed individual and I enjoyed my morning with him very much. Not only did he show me all through the Escorial, but he also gave me many interesting highlights and sidelights on the present situation in Spain and the events of the last few years from the fall of the monarchy to the rise of Franco.

The Escorial is truly a stupendous monument, a worthy memorial to Philip II, the King of Spain who constructed it. Built toward the end of the sixteenth century, this vast structure comprises a palace, a church, a mausoleum, a college, and a monastery. It is a work of art in itself and contains many works of art. It is built in the form of a gridiron to symbolize the manner of the martyrdom of St. Lawrence, to whom it is dedicated.

We arrived in the Palace chapel which is really a great church. From altar to choir loft, from dome to crypt, the lines and effects are awesome. We were there during the celebration of Solemn High Mass. Everything about the ceremony was impressive. After Mass we visited the crypts beneath the high altar to see the tombs of Emperors, Kings and Queens of Spain, of Bourbons and Hapsburgs. Monuments of beautiful marble and bronze fill the spacious rooms in the crypt. Only one tomb remains empty. It is located in the main chamber, directly beneath the high altar, and is the tomb destined to receive the remains of Alfonso XIII, the last King of Spain, or at least the latest. I had met Alfonso three times, once as a king and twice in exile. He certainly could not have had much happiness in being king. On one of his visits to the Escorial, Alfonso scratched these words with his sword on the bronze plaque of this black marble tomb: "This is my burial place." Perhaps it will be his tomb, but his body now rests in Rome, where he died.

The last time I met Alfonso was in London in 1932, one year after he had fled from Spain and the Spanish Republic had been established. As you will remember, I was then secretary to Cardinal Lauri, the Papal Legate to the Eucharistic Congress in Dublin. We were returning to Rome after the Congress, and when we reached London, the ex-king asked to call on the Cardinal to pay his respects. Alfonso was alone. His family was scattered. He was not only alone, but he was also a lonely, pathetic figure, made more so by his apparent efforts to be cheerful. One of the advantages of democracies over monarchies and dictatorships is that it is possible to lose one's position without also losing one's country.

The Escorial is kept in excellent condition and order. The rooms of Philip II, plain and austere, still contain his personal belongings. In contrast to the austere character of his own quarters, he made the church strikingly beautiful. His rooms are in direct communication with the church, and from them he could view the altar.

The library of the Escorial is another object of great interest. Here we had the good fortune of being accompanied by the old librarian, an Augustinian Father, who loves his work and his books and certainly knows a great deal about them. This is one of the world's most valuable libraries. Its nucleus was the private collection of four thousand volumes given by Philip II. The Arabic, Greek, and Latin manuscripts gathered here are said to be of extraordinary value. In the main hall of the library, there are five large tables of porphyry and jasper, with great cases containing the most precious of these treasures. Among them is the famous eleventh-century "Codex Aureus," called thus because the Gospels are lettered in gold. I saw also richly illuminated breviaries, books from which every priest recites prescribed prayers, and missals, books used to follow the Mass.

After visiting the Escorial we had luncheon and then, with some friends of former years, I went to other places of interest. In the evening, with Ambassador and Mrs. Hayes, I went to dinner as the guest of the Ambassador from Portugal to Spain. The other two guests were the British Ambassador, Sir Samuel Hoare, and Lady Maud.

On Sunday morning, Ambassador and Mrs. Hayes went with me to the Cathedral for Mass. I certainly received every attention. The Cathedral clergy expected me to be twice as large in stature as I am, and then they must have made still further allowances, for the alb and the other vestments all but smothered me. After I had finished Mass, the Vicar General and the canons kindly explained to me things of particular interest in the Cathedral.

In the afternoon, the Ambassador went with me to Toledo. All along the way one could see the effects of the war. The visit to the ruins of the Alcazar depressed me, for I remember the palace in all its glory. On this peaceful Sunday afternoon, I heard the story of fifteen hundred men, women, and children who were besieged there. I saw the ruins of the magnificent building and the room, used as both chapel and hospital, where operations were performed without anaesthesia. I saw the place where were entombed in closets, in standing position, the bodies of one hundred and four persons who had died. I looked at the remains of the graceful courtyard of the Alcazar, and tried to understand what had happened and why it had happened. The world volcano of hate is still in full eruption, still pouring forth lava of hatred, spreading it over the world.

One of the gripping incidents connected with the defense of the Alcazar concerns a Commander of the garrison, Colonel Moscardo. He was the leader of the fifteen hundred men, women, and children, who were either Monarchists, or espousers of the cause of Franco, or both. The Loyalists seized Colonel Moscardo's son and forced him to telephone to his father in the Alcazar that they would shoot him if his father did not surrender. Colonel Moscardo told his son over the telephone, "If you must die, give your soul to God; cry 'Long live Spain!' and die as a patriot." Louis Moscardo, eighteen years of age, was shot on July 23, 1936. The words of Colonel Moscardo are inscribed on a tablet in the midst of the ruins. The Alcazar was destroyed but it never surrendered. "We deliver to you the Alcazar in ruins," said Colonel Moscardo to General Franco, "but our honor is intact."

From the Alcazar, we proceeded to the Cathedral of Toledo, one of the finest churches in Spain and one of the world's grandest cathedrals. It is of Gothic design. The original building was begun by St. Eugene, first Archbishop of Toledo, the patron saint of Pope Pius XII. The passing centuries have bequeathed to the church many and varied works of art. In this old and venerable shrine, I saw, in long rows and tiers, the tombs of Toledo's Archbishops. As I looked upon them, I thought of the comparative youth of the Church in New York, for the tombs of New York's Archbishops in the crypt of St. Patrick's Cathedral thus far are but five.

After our visit to the Cathedral, we called on Archbishop Pla y Daniel, the Primate of Spain. The Archbishop has been recently transferred to Toledo from Salamanca. He is a man in his late sixties, small in stature, very cordial in manner, clear and quick in mind and in speech. He is reputedly one of the most scholarly members of the Spanish Hierarchy. At my request he gave me three of his pastoral letters. For over an hour he talked with us about the present-day situation in Spain. I think he has —I know he has—a tremendous task confronting him, tremendous in many aspects. His diocese is vast; many of his priests have been martyred; and, in addition to religious cares, he has worries in regard to affairs temporal and material.

There are things about Spain that are difficult to understand; but then, I suppose, there are things about every country that a foreigner has difficulty in understanding. I have been twice before in Spain, both times when Spain was a monarchy. I have spoken with many persons and read many articles about Spain. There is the widest divergence in reports about what happened in Spain, why it happened, how it happened. I have also sought opinions from Spaniards and non-Spaniards about the future of Spain. They have discussed the attitude of the Spanish people toward the war, toward the return of the monarchy, toward the Allies and Axis nations, and toward America. I am unable, however, to have a clear and complete picture of the whole situation, past, present, and future. The past is clouded. The present and future are foggy. The clouds and fogs are essentially the same, and both are tinged with red and not with the red of the sunrise. Spain is definitely war-weary, but the spirit of war is smouldering. The wounds of civil war are deep, festering and difficult to heal.

Generalissimo Franco is in the middle of all. Some are favorable to him, some opposed; some partly favorable, some partly opposed. Most of the people that I met are supporters of Franco. His supporters say that the Generalissimo is striving to keep Spain out of the war and this policy is approved by large numbers of persons who believe Spain has had enough war for this generation.

Spain's attitude toward the United States has improved immeasurably during the past twelve months, as I learned from sources other than our Ambassador. This change in feeling was at least partially due to the fact that America sent petroleum and cotton to Spain and both products are vitally needed by the Spaniards. As a consequence, the Spanish people have liked us better. There is a very strict control of petroleum so that none of it can reach the Axis Powers. Thus, by improving our country's relations with Spain, Dr. Hayes fulfills the mission expected of an Ambassador. Some persons criticize this policy as appeasement. Certainly, the life of an ambassador, any ambassador, is not an easy one at the present time. In war time the position of a representative from a belligerent country to a neutral one is extremely difficult. It is impossible to satisfy every one, and sometimes one is tempted to think that it is almost impossible to satisfy any one. An ambassador is every man's football. If things go well, then they would go well anyway even if there were no ambassador. If he does something which is not approved by one or another group, he is denounced. If he secures some concession from his own country for the country to which he is accredited, he may be accused of being an "appeaser" or of acting on grounds of "expediency." The inexorable implication is that an appeasement is something inherently evil, and that an expedient thing cannot be a good thing.

Groups called "Liberals" and "Republicans" assumed power in Spain at the time when King Alfonso XIII fled, and in a general election were confirmed in power. In 1936, the two political parties called themselves "Loyalists" and "Nationalists." The term "Loyalist" is equivocally used in Spain and in America. Considering what the name ordinarily connotes, any one would instinctively give sympathy and support to a group of "loyalists." However some Spaniards do not call the members of this group "Loyalists." They call them "Communists." The "Nationalists" under General Franco maintained that they would have been able to have assumed control over Spain if international legionnaires had not come to the aid of the "Loyalists." On the other side Nazi Germany and Fascist Italy sent help to Franco. Whatever and however all this happened, this much is sure—Spain lost, and lost desperately.

There are many Spaniards who desire a return of the monarchy and are in agreement more and more now than formerly, for the pretender to the throne has married a Carlist, which unites in one family both groups desirous of monarchical rule.

The Republican-Loyalist-Communist coalition called itself Democratic. It favored "reform." Spain needed reform and so does every nation and person. But whatever they were for, they were certainly against the clergy. In Madrid alone, they killed seven hundred priests. Eleven Spanish bishops throughout the country perished also. Others besides the Loyalists were opposed to Franco. The Basques and the Catalonians were against him because they were separatists and wished their own independence from Spain. Chaos was everywhere. People were stopped on the streets and asked to which party they belonged; if they gave the wrong answer, they were shot. Thousands were put to death for no greater crime than wearing a necktie, because that custom indicated that they belonged to the middle class, and were therefore definitely against the working people.

Hatred of religion and its manifestations approximated an hysterical high point. Cruelties paralleled those inflicted on the martyrs of the early Church. On the so-called "Hill of the Angels," which is in the geographic center of Spain, there is a large statue of the Sacred Heart of Jesus. Fanatical hatred of Christ and Christ's religion reached such a point that a firing squad "executed" the statue. When Franco gained control of Spain in 1939, thousands of Spaniards were cast into prison. Many of them are there to this day. Naturally, the prisoners are very bitter; the relatives of the slain on both sides are bitter; and domestic hatreds in Spain are very deep. No family has been spared suffering and death, and the streets are filled with women dressed in mourning.

Like pestilences, fires, avalanches, religious and racial hatreds kill, burn, and sweep onwards. "Hodie mihi; cras tibi," Christians and Jews may say to one another. "Today, me; tomorrow, you," is true of more things than death. Self-interest, as well as mutual sympathy, should unite Jews, Christians, all nationalties, all peoples in common efforts for justice and peace.

I have tried to give you something of the picture of Spain as

I saw it. It is a distressed country and needs help, help from other countries, but also help from herself. With economic assistance, with social reforms, with extensions of liberties to all the people, with education, with religion, I hope and pray that peace and prosperity may come to the Spanish people.

At dinner on Sunday evening, I met Colonel Hohenthal, Military Attaché to the American Embassy, lately returned from Africa.

The following day, February 15th, Ambassador Hayes accompanied me to meet Count Jordana, the Minister of Foreign Affairs. I found him to be deeply interested in America. We had dinner at the Nunciature. The Nuncio, Archbishop Cicognani, had as other guests Bishop Leopoldo Eijo y Garay of Madrid, Bishop Gregorio Cassus of Barcelona, and bishops from several other places. During the dinner I thought several times of a remark made to me by a man familiar with Spain, a remark that was striking and terrifying: "Twenty-four hours of disorder in Spain," he said, "could mean the assassination of every bishop, priest, and nun that could be found." It is startling to realize that one is in the company of possible martyrs. One authority states that more than fifteen thousand priests and about the same number of nuns were killed in Spain during the Civil War. The Bishop of Madrid, by the narrowest margin, escaped the clutches of those who were intent on crucifying him in one of the squares of Madrid. When I visited him, he showed me a crucifix above his bed with bullet holes through the body of Christ.

On Monday afternoon, I attended a meeting of a group of American and Spanish women in a house called "Casa Americana." These women, under the presidency of Mrs. Hayes, knit, sew and do other works for charitable purposes. Leaving this little assembly, I returned to the Embassy where I was informed that Generalissimo Franco was to receive me the next day.

By way of preparation for the audience with General Franco, I read the address given by President Roosevelt on Lincoln's Birthday at the annual meeting of the White House Correspondents' Association in Washington. I also re-read Ambassador Hayes' address on "America's War Aims."

I went alone to the Prado Palace and arrived shortly after midday. I was saluted by a company of soldiers, and escorted up a flight of stairs to a large waiting room, beautifully furnished in the usual Spanish style for palaces, with Goya-designed and Madrid-executed tapestries of a century ago, and also a rug, evidently made expressly for the room, bearing the date of 1825. The room was provided with the usual great number of tables, chairs and mirrors around the sides of the wall, rock crystal chandeliers, and normally equipped with clocks to the number of three. I did not have more than a moment to glance around when Baron de Las Torres, the Chief of Protocol, came into the room, and in a minute or two we went back across the hall, through another waiting room, and, on the opening of double doors, were in the presence of the Generalissimo.

His room is large but not unduly so, and the walls are covered with red damask. He was seated at a desk at the end of the room opposite the door. There were high windows along the side on the right hand of the entrance. He left his desk and came forward to meet me, and motioned me to a seat and he himself took a chair with his back to the window.

I had been told by some who had known him all through his life that the Generalissimo was a God-fearing, serious and intelligent man, striving to do what he thought was best for Spain.

He seems to be brimming over with health and energy, and his desk, stacked high with folders and papers, reminded me of my own. During the entire discussion, he talked in Spanish and I talked in Italian. We understood each other easily. He smiled half a dozen times during the conversation which I mention because I had never seen a picture of him smiling.

The conversation pivoted on the international situation and the war. We covered a great deal of territory, and in time we went from the Treaty of Versailles down to the present, and we did not stop there. We ventured a few thoughts about the future. I explained the American point of view as well as I could, motivated by facts and examples.

Naturally, the Generalissimo understood that I spoke to him as a private American citizen, intensely interested in and devoted to the welfare of my country, and as a priest, interested in and devoted to the spiritual and temporal welfare of all peoples.

As I took my leave, the Generalissimo again expressed his admiration for America and wished me a happy journey.

From the Prado Palace, I went directly to the house of the Bishop of Madrid for luncheon. The Apostolic Nuncio, Monsignor Cicognani, Ambassador Hayes and others were present.

One learns about a country much more easily and lastingly by visiting it and talking to various people than in any other way. Geography is so helpful to history, and some knowledge of geography has helped me in this high-pressure course in the history of Spain. It is a sad, complicated history, especially in its civil wars. A great deal of super-patriotism, super-charity, and super-good-sense is needed in Spain by all. Some might think it could all be solved by saying: "Let every one be free, just as every one in the United States is free, and then everything will be just fine." This formula for freedom is not so simple in its immediate application in our sense in every place in the world. Freedom is an anomalous term. To some, it means opportunities to be brutal, to rob, and to kill.

Before the recent civil war, Spain was in a relatively prosperous condition, but there has been so much destruction, so much civil unrest, and so many people killed that the country is distressed and depressed. National peace must be the first prelude to prosperity. The death toll of the Spanish civil war was seven hundred thousand lives lost in battle, thirty thousand by execution or assassination, and fifteen thousand as the result of air raids. I was told that in the city of Barcelona eighty thousand people were slain, and from the Madrid airport, I saw a cross which marks the location of trenches where lay the bodies of three thousand Nationalists who were executed by the Loyalists in two days.

I spent the last afternoon in Madrid by myself. I was saddened by all that I had seen and heard, and I decided that I would like to be alone for a while. I went to the Prado Gallery and wandered through its rooms of masterpieces. Afterwards I walked to the Franciscan Church to meditate and pray. It is very easy to pray when one is sad and I remained in the church a long time. I then returned to the Embassy and had a pleasant meeting with the members of the staff and other Americans who live in Madrid.

On Wednesday, February 17th, Ambassador Hayes went with me to the airport. The Nuncio was there to bid me good-bye, and also Monsignor Clarizio, who was to go on the same plane with me to Rome. The plane was very late and I begged the Ambassador and the Nuncio to leave. Most kindly, but I am sure with much sacrifice, did they insist on remaining until the plane left Madrid for Barcelona some four hours behind the time of its scheduled departure.

The trip from Lisbon to Madrid had been so very stormy that a rough journey from Madrid to Barcelona was anticipated. When we left, snow was falling in Madrid, a rare occurrence. Quite unexpectedly, therefore, we had a very pleasant trip to Barcelona, the capital of the Catalonian province of Spain. The plane was an Italian Savoia-Marchetti, and seated eighteen passengers. All the passengers looked at all the other passengers and wondered, for no traveler on any airplane, at least any airplane flying over Europe, is traveling just for fun.

I sat with Monsignor Clarizio and chatted with him. Time was not long until, for the first time in many years, I thrilled to see the beautiful blue of the Mediterranean as we reached it just above Tarragona.

In Barcelona we met Mr. Makinson, the American Consul General, who has been in the Consular service for many years. We talked of Spain, and of Japan, where he was located at the time of the attack on Pearl Harbor. We dined together, and kept on talking until well after midnight.

During our stay in Barcelona, Monsignor Clarizio and I said Mass at the Jesuit Church. We visited the Church at various hours, and at all times found it well filled with devout people. Many men were in the congregation.

We learned that the departure of the airplane for Rome was delayed, and so we went sight-seeing. We visited the Cathedral where priests who were candidates for the office of canon were delivering prepared sermons before the other canons. I listened for a time and I congratulated myself that I had no more examinations to take in this world. More important than taking examinations, however, is making them of one's self to prepare for life's final examination.

We went to the City Hall and to the Provincial Chamber of Deputies. In the City Hall there is a striking room called "Sala de las Cronicas." The paintings are by Sert, an artist well known in America. He is a Catalonian by birth and Spaniards are very proud of him.

I met several old friends in Barcelona, among them Father Isasi, a Carmelite priest, who for many years was stationed in the United States. I met also some Republicans and Loyalists. One very sincere young man was most frank. According to him "hunger" is Communism's chief food in Spain. There are about one and a quarter million people in Barcelona and of this number only about fifty thousand are well-off; the rest have a great struggle to survive. The young man cited an instance of a family consisting of a husband, his wife, and child, and his mother-in-law. They live in a hovel. The rent is actually small but it is great to them because they cannot pay it. The husband has been without work for some time. In order to keep the family from starvation, the women have been making aprons at the rate of ten centimes each, about two cents in United States currency. By working from daybreak until well along in the night, the three women are able to make between seventy-five cents and a dollar a day. With this amount the whole family tries to subsist. If, instead of two cents per apron, the women could receive ten cents each for them, the family might buy sufficient food and clothing, and pay their rent. There are thousands of similar sad situations. Economic helps as well as economic adjustments are necessary, together with common sense, justice, and charity. Although conditions are definitely acute, nothing is hopeless and nothing should be so regarded any time, anywhere. Anything can happen, and why not, through the grace of God, hope for something good!

I was delayed a second day in Barcelona and I went to visit Mount Tibidabo, imaginatively considered as the place where our Lord was tempted. From the mountain top there is a tremendous vista of surrounding countryside and the Mediterranean. "Tibidabo" means "I will give to you," the words of Satan tempting Christ in His human nature as he showed Him the vision of all the kingdoms of the world. I had happiest recollections of my previous trip to this site and of my visit to Montserrat, "Lohengrin's" monastery, which was clearly visible across the valley on another range of mountains.

Everywhere I go, I see the present on the background of the past; and, as from Tibidabo I looked down at Barcelona and over the Mediterranean, I dreamed a bit. There were many things to dream about, thousands of years of things in times gone by and things that lie ahead. What progress man has made in many things! But in fundamental things the balance sheet is red, red with man's blood—with heroes' blood and martyrs' blood.

"There are no atheists in fox holes." How can there be atheists anywhere? How can death be "the be-all and the end-all" for those valiant men now fighting, dying for a cause they believe to be just! How can death be "the be-all and the end-all" of lives lived nobly for a cause! If there be no God, who or what is the great first cause? What and where is nature's motor? Who made nature's always-identically-operating laws? Who gave the spark of life to men? Who gave a soul to man; a mind to think, to understand; a will to do or not to do? If God be not, wherein the sanction of man's deeds, wherein the difference between men's lives lived well and lived as beasts?

On the afternoon of the same day, I attended a meeting held for the benefit of the Allied soldiers. I spoke on the work of the Chaplains in the war. That evening we were told that the plane would leave Barcelona for Rome early the next morning.

Monsignor Clarizio and myself celebrated Mass at the Jesuit Church before six o'clock. Mr. and Mrs. Makinson and the Vice Consul, Mr. Caragol, accompanied us to the airport. All formalities, including a medical visit, were made very easy for us. For one reason or another we did not board the plane until ten o'clock. While we were waiting, I had the unpleasant experience of witnessing the departure of an American-manufactured airplane bearing the Nazi emblem, taking off for Stuttgart and Berlin. It was one of a number of Dutch aircraft captured by the Germans when they struck Holland.

Our plane was crowded with passengers and baggage. I was the only enemy alien on board. Every one, including members of the crew and the passengers, was most considerate.

The trip was beautiful and to me most thought-provoking. Imagine flying over Corsica with Sardinia visible to the south! Within half an hour, we passed above Ajaccio, Corsica, the birthplace of Napoleon, and Elba, the place of his exile. But what events occurred in the lifetime of Napoleon between Ajaccio and Elba! His career flashed before my mind as in a cinema. I thought of Napoleon's modern counterpart who has set on fire and ravaged the modern world. I visualized him as he looked down on Napoleon's tomb in Paris, after his Nazi legions had devastated Poland and western Europe from the Baltic to the Pyrenees, and I thought of the first time I had looked at that tomb of Napoleon. It was in 1911, and as I stood beneath the dome of the Invalides and gazed on the porphyry mausoleum that contains the body of Napoleon, I heard a Frenchman say: "I curse that man who was the curse of France! I curse him for the lives he took, the lives that never lived on his account, for the inch he took from the height of Frenchmen who lived after him!" What did Hitler think when he saw Napoleon's tomb? Whatever he thought, he makes me think of anti-Christ. Never before has any one sown so widely, so thickly, and so deeply the dragon's teeth of hatred and cruelty.

We passed Caprera with its memories of Garibaldi, and then the isle of Monte Cristo. Now, with heart action a little quicker, I see the shores of Italy. Moving with the speed of light, memory flashes a pageant of my Roman days, twelve years of life. Civita Vecchia, Bracciano, Ivanhoe's Castle, and now St. Peter's dome! Eleven years away from it and yet but yesterday it seems! We are flying low; it is easy to pick out familiar places—but oh! we are going so fast. We are already coming down to the airport of Littorio which I left so many years ago on the first flight of my life—to Venice, Vienna, Budapest, Bucharest, Sofia, Belgrade, Istanbul, Athens, and back to Rome! And he who bade me good-bye the day I began that journey, he who has been always a loyal, devoted friend, Enrico Galeazzi, is there to welcome me. For the moment everything is wonderful. I am happy. But the pressure of realities soon bursts through my happiness. Things seem strange and persons seem so sad. I am an enemy. I am in an enemy country. The Italians are my enemies. They are enemies of my country. It all seems so weird and wrong.

I was stunned. Realizing everything, I could realize nothing.

With everything familiar, I moved in an unfamiliar world. I was told to get into an automobile. I did so. The automobile started. I was told that I was to go to the American College on the Janiculum Hill which Italy considers extra-territorial. I said I wanted to go to St. Peter's, and we went to St. Peter's!

I got out of the car. Friends and acquaintances of years ago greeted me. Others recognized and welcomed me. I walked up the steps and entered St. Peter's. I was home. I prayed before the tomb of St. Peter, where I offered my first Mass as a priest; and before the altar of the chair of St. Peter, where I was consecrated a bishop. I walked about the Basilica, thinking, praying, sorrowful in my happiness, happy in my sorrow. Mr. Galeazzi told me that it was time to go to the American College, but before I went, I made arrangements to celebrate Mass at the tomb of St. Peter the following morning, Sunday, February 21st. This also was an emotional experience. For the living and dead I prayed, and for the rescue of humanity. After Mass I said prayers at the tombs of the Popes that I had known: Pius X, Benedict XV, and Pius XI, and also for Cardinal Merry del Val.

I was told that I was invited to attend a meeting of the Pontifical Academy of Science that morning, over which the Holy Father was to preside, and that after the meeting, I was to be received in audience.

I arrived early for the meeting and met a great many friends. Suddenly, five minutes before the appointed time, the door opened. A hush came over the assembly, and there was Pope Pius XII!

The Holy Father has aged with more than years since last I saw him when he was Cardinal Pacelli. The countless sorrows that had throbbed in his heart had also etched his face with grief and care.

I thought of last Christmas and the Pope's message which I read just before the Midnight Mass in St. Patrick's, words which touched me deeply, words well understandable but not understood for the most part except by those for whom he had prayed and pleaded—"the sorrowing hosts of mothers, widows and orphans, numberless exiles and hundreds of thousands of persons, who without any fault on their part, sometimes only because of their nationality or race, had been consigned to death."

That was the night on which again the Pope protested that international agreement to make war less inhuman by confining it to combatants had remained a dead letter. That was the time when he prayed and pleaded for a return of the world to its "center of gravity," which is God's law. That was yet another time that he denounced, as he had from the beginning, the horrors of indiscriminate bombings of non-combatants—women, children, sick and aged, hospitals, charitable institutions and houses of prayer.

On many occasions, the Pope has proclaimed his impartial love for all peoples. Naturally, His Holiness thinks of the sufferings of the weak and the lowly. To them he is very close and devoted.

The Christmas message of the Pope I read again, but this time it was a wordless message in his eyes.

The Holy Father looked at me smilingly and then went to his chair. All was quiet. He began to speak. Of the discourse itself I shall not write, for it was published in America in its entirety. In his characteristically beautiful style, the Holy Father spoke for half an hour. As always, he used no manuscript and delivered his address just as he had written it.

After the meeting of the Academy, the Pope greeted the twelve Cardinals who were present and then came to me as I knelt waiting for his approach. He placed his hands on my shoulders, bade me rise, welcomed me, and told me to accompany him. I was with His Holiness about two hours. Afterwards I remained in the Vatican and talked with Mr. Galeazzi until five o'clock, when I again went to the Holy Father. It was eight o'clock before I returned to the Villa after a day that I shall never forget.

The Holy Father thinks of the war all the time, and all the time he works and prays for peace. Just before the outbreak of hostilities in 1939, he addressed a most fervent plea to the rulers of nations and peoples. "Nothing," he said, "is lost by peace. All can be lost by war." What the Pope visualized and what he warned would happen has happened. His fears have proved to be all too true! Those who counted on a quick military triumph are now contemplating, or should contemplate, the grim specter of defeat, and their own ignominious end.

No one understands more clearly than the Pope the horror and the devastation of war, and of this war. No one suffers more poignantly, more deeply than he. He feels the sorrows of all. He sees the blood and the tears of all. He sees tremendous masses of men increasingly efficient in mutual massacre, increasingly enmeshed by tentacles of brutality and hate. He realizes that hate begets hate, that brutality spawns brutality and that revenge cries for revenge. The juggernaut of war crushes forward and backward over nations and peoples. Men aflame with savage goadings rush onward crashing other men aflame and thus the conflagration mounts, spreads, devastates and consumes.

The Pope thinks, works, prays and literally dies for peace. He wishes the conquerors to be not only just with the conquered but also merciful. He knows full well that revenge is a bitter, gnawing thing. "All nations, great and small," he says, "have a right to live." He exhorts nations and their rulers to make their actions agree with their principles. The leaders of conquering nations will have opportunities to show not only greatness in victory but also greatness in making the peace. Our leaders have stated our war aims and our peace aims. The Holy Father hopes that peace and justice will come in conformity with the principles that have been proclaimed, and the strongest guarantee of lasting peace will be justice tempered with charity.

That evening I had supper with Monsignor Brennan of Philadelphia, Monsignor Carroll of Pittsburgh, and Monsignor MacGeough of New York. They have positions in different offices of the Holy See, and all of them reside in the Villa. I had been informed that the Italian Government would permit me to go anywhere I would desire. However, I preferred to remain in the Vatican or at the Villa. The Cardinals were all gracious enough to come to see me, since by my self-imposed restrictions I could not call on them. I also saw every American priest and nun living in Rome and made note of their home addresses so that I might contact their relatives as soon as I returned to America, and say that I had seen them. I had conversations with many old and dear friends. I was able to care for many official matters pertaining to the Church in the United States, which for months had been awaiting disposition.

On Washington's Birthday I attended a reception at the home of our American representative to the Vatican, Mr. Harold Tittman. All Americans stationed at the Vatican were present and also all the American members of various Religious Orders, members of the diplomatic corps and representatives to the Holy See from the South American countries were present. I talked with the representatives at the Vatican of all the allied countries. Several times I met Mr. D'Arcy Osborne, the British Minister to the Holy See; Mr. Kiernan, the Irish Minister; Mr. Papée, the Polish Minister, and Mr. Kang Sie Cheou of China. I neither spoke with nor saw the representatives of Germany, Italy, or Japan.

I spent much time at the Vatican Information Office for War Prisoners, and also attended the meeting of the Council for the Distribution of War Relief. The Pope is deeply interested in the work of the Vatican Information Office. Some governments are not favorable to this activity of the Holy See but the mothers and wives of the soldiers "missing in action" appreciate the service. It seems as though there are some who think that the International Red Cross should have the exclusive privilege of giving information about persons who are prisoners of war, but the Vatican thinks that, in no spirit of competition with the Red Cross but only in a spirit of cooperation in doing good, it should have the opportunity to secure and give out information in this regard, wherever it is possible. The Holy Father has directed that information concerning prisoners be communicated by telegram whenever this method is available, to lessen days of distress and sorrow. The Holy See is doing everything that its means permit to help the prisoners of war. I presented to the Pope the Peter's Pence offering of the clergy and faithful of the Archdiocese of New York. It amounted this year to fifty thousand dollars. The Holy Father directed that this sum be used at once in its entirety to help the prisoners of war of all nations.

It is impossible to mention the names of all those I saw and the great variety of things I was asked to do. It seemed as if any one with any problem of any kind came to me for a solution. And these days every one has some problem.

I visited the work that has been done in the Basilica of St. Peter's and in the Vatican. Important archeological discoveries have recently been made, and I felt like a student again as things were explained to me. I also saw the first showing of the film version of the life of the Holy Father. Its title is "Pastor Angelicus."

The many precious hours I had with the Holy Father reminded me of other years, happier years, when I was privileged to be in his company, when we worked, talked, walked and prayed together. I thought of the many times I had assisted him as he offered Mass. I thought also of the visit of His Holiness to America, of being with him on his visit to President Roosevelt, and of having the honor of receiving him in the parish house in Newton Center, Massachusetts, and also at our home in Whitman. Again I was privileged to be with him, see him, talk with him, pray with him at night in his private chapel where he led the rosary and I answered.

My farewell audience with the Holy Father was yesterday, March 2nd, his sixty-seventh birthday and the fourth anniversary of his election as Pope. At this audience His Holiness gave me the cross and chain which he had received on the day of his consecration as Archbishop, twenty-five years ago, and which he has worn ever since. I do not like to take it with me on this journey, but I will do so, and wear it constantly.

Early this morning I said my last Mass at the Villa, using the chalice loaned to me by the Holy Father for use during my stay in Rome. I prayed God to spare him to the Church and begged blessings on my country and my countrymen. With Mr. Galeazzi and the American priests with whom I lived during my eleven days' stay in Rome, I left for the Guidonia Airport.

I did not take a direct route as I wished to go by the old buildings of the North American College in Via dell' Umilta to say a prayer for my classmates and friends of my student years. On the way to the airport we went by the church and cemetery of San Lorenzo. A few formalities, a few minutes for farewells, and once more I am aboard a plane for the seven-hour flight to Seville. I had arrived in Rome circling over the north, but this time we were sweeping by the southern part of the city, passing over St. John Lateran, the Mother of all Churches, the Coliseum, over St. Paul's, following the Ostian Way and the Tiber River. Once again I am over the blue Mediterranean. I kept my gaze fixed backwards for many minutes just as long as I could still see St. Peter's Dome suspended above the lightest veil of mist, apart from the world.

Once more Sardinia and Corsica, the Balearic Islands, Majorca, Minorca, and on to the coast of Spain near Valencia, over Cordoba, following the Guadalquivir River to Seville.

Spain again! The American Consul, Mr. John Hamlin, was at the airport. He cordially invited me to be the guest of Mrs. Hamlin and himself and I gratefully accepted his invitation.

Mr. Hamlin accompanied me to see Cardinal Segura, the Archbishop of Seville. After a most cordial visit to the Cardinal, Mr. Hamlin returned to the Consulate and I went into the Cathedral for an hour. It is vast—the fifth or sixth largest Cathedral in the world. I returned there for Mass both mornings I spent in Seville. The altar on which I offered the Holy Sacrifice was beside the tomb of San Fernando, King of Spain, who died in 1298. The main altar is before a reredos, and fifty or sixty feet above it rises a beautiful heavily sculptured dome. On every visit to the Cathedral I saw more of its treasures—sacred vestments, reliquaries, sacred vessels, and other objects, including an ivory crucifix with the hands of our Lord stretching directly upward because the crucifix was carved in one piece from an ivory tusk.

I saw the tomb of Columbus who, after his return from the discovery of the new world, was received here with honors on Palm Sunday, 1493. I saw, also, the building called the Archives of the Indies, where there are memorials of Columbus, documents with the signature of Pizarro, Cortez, Magellan, Cervantes, Balboa, and Amerigo Vespucci. It is one of the world's greatest collections. I was introduced to an old lady there, Miss Alice Gould. I knew that she was an American and I asked her from what part of the States she came. She answered, "Quincy, Massachusetts." She was amazed when I said, "I am from Whitman, Massachusetts." Tears came to her eyes. She has been away from home for thirty years, studying archives in Spain, and is one of the foremost authorities on Columbus. John Adams and John Quincy Adams were among her ancestors. I told her that I knew the house in which she said she was born. We forgot Columbus and Spain and were back in Massachusetts. Mr. and Mrs. Hamlin were kind enough to invite her to dinner so that we could talk longer together of our homeland.

On Friday, March 5th, I left Seville by automobile for Gibraltar. The day was beautiful. The countryside around Seville, because of its fertility, is known as the land of the Blessed Virgin. The road was excellent and I had time to gather my thoughts and meditate a bit. As I drove in peace and quiet down through southern Spain the predominant prayer was that God might save man from himself and inspire him to help himself, his neighbor, and the human race, instead of killing his neighbor and destroying and ravaging.

The city of Cadiz, the Venice of Spain, was not directly on my route but I had never been there before and wanted to see it. We drove through its principal streets. We stopped at a place along the harbor front, and sitting on the sea wall, gazing at the Atlantic Ocean, the chauffeur and I ate our luncheon together. Though eggs are a great luxury, we each had one. Eggs are rationed in nearly every country, one egg per person per month being the allotment in Italy. However, a ration is one thing but it is quite another thing to get the egg.

I continued my journey down to the edge of Spain. Cape Trafalgar, the scene of Nelson's great victory over the French and the Spanish, was in the distance. Along the oceanside we passed great pyramids of salt, for the salt used in Spain is obtained from sea water by evaporation processes.

I reached the border town of La Linea where Spain meets Gibraltar. I was met by Major Capuro, representing the Governor General, Commander O'Brien of the United States Navy, and Colonel Holcomb of the United States Army. They told me that I was to be the guest of His Excellencey, Lieutenant General Mason MacFarlane, the Governor General of Gibraltar. The Governor General welcomed me at the Government House. Two centuries ago this residence was a convent. It was called "the Convent" down through the years until the early part of this century. The change in name from Convent to Government House was occasioned by a visit of King Edward VII to Gibraltar. The King was the guest of the Governor and it was reported in the British newspapers that the King had luncheon with the Governor General at "the Convent." A religious group wrote to the King expressing wonder that he would visit a convent and more than wonder that he would have luncheon there. The King then changed the name to Government House. There is a letter on the mantlepiece in the reception room which refers to this incident. General Mason MacFarlane invited General Hallinan, Commander of the armed forces in Gibraltar, and Bishop Fitzgerald to dinner. Gibraltar's governor is always a General and, therefore, his title is Governor General. Other British possessions have governors who are nonmilitary, and their title is simply "Governor." General Mason MacFarlane has served in India, Germany, Austria, Bavaria, Hungary, and Russia. He is an exceptional linguist.

The following morning General Hallinan accompanied me

to visit the fortress. He showed me all the installations, numbers of new tunnels, and great reservoirs. Gibraltar has no water from springs or wells and, for a long time, the only supply obtainable was rain water collected from the natural watersheds formed of the rock or from roofs of houses. Now there is a distillation apparatus which can produce sufficient water for thousands of people. Even the hospital, recreation rooms and the barracks are cut from the solid rock. From the top I looked down at the new airfield. I saw also the harbor and many ships, some of them very well known.

The last time I was in Gibraltar was on the maiden trip of the *Rex* in 1932 when I was returning to America after my consecration as Auxiliary Bishop of Boston. Everything has greatly changed. Gibraltar is a crowded, hectic place. No women or children are permitted to live there. Many military men from England and all her dominions, colonies, and other possessions, may be seen in the streets. Traffic is very difficult in the narrow lanes. Sounding of automobile horns is prohibited and signals are made by beating with one's hand on the side of the auto door. Many Spanish people are employed in Gibraltar and crowds go back and forth to work, for all must return to Spain every night. Each person is allowed to take a ration of bread home with him. This ration is the most important wage factor, for food means much more than money.

The sun was just rising as we took off from Gibraltar, skirted the Spanish coast for a while, and then flew over the Mediterranean and followed the African coastline. On arrival at my destination, I was received by Honorable Robert Murphy, the President's special envoy and civil affairs officer in North Africa. I knew Mr. Murphy before, and he and his housemates, Colonel Holmes, Colonel Gaylord, and Colonel Spofford received me most cordially in their home.

Mr. Murphy took me to call on General Eisenhower at his headquarters. It was, of course, an honor and a privilege for me to meet the Commanding General of all the Allied Forces in North Africa. The General is a very vigorous, dynamic individual. He is a person as well as a soldier. He radiates confidence. Naturally, in his position, he must have outstanding ability in directing matters of the greatest magnitude, and to him no one person or detail is insignificant or unimportant. General Eisenhower has directed that wherever possible American and British officers of the same rank and similar services ("opposite numbers") live together for thus they know one another better and work more closely together. His energetic, efficient Chief of Staff, General "Beadle" Smith, was present at this meeting. Even one, like myself, who understands little about military affairs has the definite impression that our destinies have been confided to able leaders, intent and sure on obtaining our objectives and men also deeply conscious of the value of human life.

After my visit to General Eisenhower, Mr. Murphy took me

to call on Sir Andrew Cunningham, the Commander-in-Chief of the Fleet. The Admiral's face is aged beyond his years but his eyes and active frame bespeak his youth. His mastery of naval strategy and warfare has made him one of the great figures of the war, and he has a still greater destiny before him. From the balcony just outside his office window, an office that in peace time was a bedroom, the Admiral has a sweeping view of the Mediterranean, that great "mare nostrum" which he did much to save for the Allies' use and which his fleets now dominate. After visiting the military authorities with Mr. Murphy, I went with Father William Walsh of St. Paul, Minnesota, Chaplain in the North American Air Force, to call on the Bishop and the Vicar General. They were pleased to see me and we passed an interesting hour together. They are most cooperative in placing their churches, halls, and all other facilities at the disposition of our soldiers.

Shortly after my arrival in North Africa, I was invited to dinner by General Giraud. There were fifteen other persons present, all of them French. His appearance, his tall figure and military bearing are familiar to you from his photographs, but what his photographs do not reveal is the depth of his eyes which convince one of his sincerity. I had read and remembered his widely published letter to Marshal Pétain, in which he gave the reasons, as he saw them, for the fall of France. He told me of his wife and children who are prisoners of the Nazis and of the extra sufferings that he knew they were enduring on his account, especially because he had escaped from a Nazi prison. But the General willingly endures soul tortures as well as bodily sufferings for the salvation and the resurrection of his beloved France.

After the dinner with General Giraud, I went to a monastery of the White Fathers where the British and American Chaplains were having a day of recollection. I remained with them some time and met them all individually. Then I began a visitation of military encampments all along the North African coastline, a visitation which brought me to all parts of Morocco and Algeria. Life was very strenuous. Sometimes I was very tired, sometimes hot, sometimes cold, sad and glad. But always was I content to be just where I was, always consoled at my experience.

Every day I flew from "somewhere to somewhere," visiting different areas and different units. I went to every hospital that was possible for me to visit, went from bed to bed and had a word or two with every boy. Some boys wanted me to write to their families saying that they were getting on well and I promised to do so. The boys were courageous and cheerful. The convalescents were anxious to rejoin their units. Those definitely unable to continue in military service were naturally anxious to return to the States as soon as possible and they faced the future with determination. America's war effort is stupendously successful and one of its outstanding phases, I think, is the care given to sick and wounded. The doctors in the service are among America's finest and while the hospitals have no marble foyers or gift shops, nevertheless they equal in equipment and efficiency the best in our land. Some of these hospitals are of brick, some of cement blocks, and others of wood. They have been built by United States engineers and are in every way adequate.

In addition to general hospitals located outside of combat zones, there are field and evacuation hospitals for service nearer to the front. In one of the latter, I met Colonel Riley of San Francisco, a brother of Reverend Stanley Riley, an army Chap-

lain believed to have been captured by the Japanese. I told
Colonel Riley that I would strive through the Vatican agencies
to get some news of his brother. An evacuation hospital is generally located in tents, "under canvas," as is said. Everything
may be packed, transported, and set up in another place within
forty-eight hours. The large number of beds in a single hospital
unit is amazing. St. Vincent's Hospital in New York has five
hundred and fifty beds; covers nearly half a city block, and goes
from six to nine stories in height. Overseas military hospitals of
this size are moved about with the greatest ease! In Colonel
Riley's evacuation hospital unit, there are facilities for six simul-
taneous operations.

I also visited a hospital conducted by a Massachusetts unit, in
which I have many friends. I had met them in Camp Blanding,
Florida, just before their departure for overseas. Nearly every
place in North Africa seems to be like Main Street in one's own
home town.

Oftentimes by myself I have gone to military cemeteries. I
remember well my visit to the Hillside Cemetery near the city
of Oran. Sometimes one sees many deaths with the same date
on the grave markers indicating groups that have died together
in a battle or in a plane crash. I went from grave to grave and
said prayers for all. In another cemetery I was pleased to see a
flower or two on every grave, and to learn from the chaplains
that not one soldier had yet died in Africa without being buried
with a religious service.

On more than one occasion chaplains have risked their lives
for men already dead. One chaplain led a squad of men to a
plane crash on a narrow shelf of mountain side to extricate the
bodies and afford them honored burial.

One of the things I had in mind to do when I left America, if it were possible, was to offer Mass at the grave of Father Falter, the first American Chaplain killed in action in North Africa. I had met Father Falter at Camp Ord in California a few months before he went overseas. The cemetery in which he is buried is in the town of Fedala, one of the places on the African coast where the American troops landed. Directly over Father Falter's grave, an altar had been erected on a platform. A large number of soldiers and sailors had been given permission to attend this Mass, which was to be offered not only for Father Falter but also for all the other soldiers and sailors buried in this cemetery.

It was a beautiful, sunshiny day. For me this was a most moving occasion under the vault of a cloudless sky in nature's great cathedral with hundreds of birds singing during the Mass. Afterwards I spoke briefly and met personally all who were present. I asked for their names and home addresses. Guarding carefully the identity of their outfit and other restricted information, I intend to contact their relatives when I return, and tell them that I saw their boys. Later, I went down to the place on the shore where Father Falter was killed.

That day I had luncheon at the residence of Governor General Noguès, whom I had met with General Giraud. This residence of the French Military Governor of Morocco was built some twenty-five or thirty years ago by General Lyautey. It is

48

spacious, impressive, well-appointed and very well maintained. There were many guests at the luncheon, including the Bishop of Rabat, the Grand Vizier and his aide, and a number of French and American officers and civilians. After luncheon Madame Noguès, who is a daughter of the former French Minister Delcassé, showed us through the house and the gardens. These gardens are really a riot of color.

During my stay in Rabat, I was a guest of General Keyes in the house which General Patton had just left for his new command. It was a beautiful villa overlooking the ocean. In war areas one can be amid luxurious comforts one day and in mud or dust the next. One General, startled to find himself in one of these villas and enjoying it, said to me, "I won't put on a hair shirt until I have to."

In Casablanca I was housed in the villa in which the President lived during the famous conference and I was shown to his room. In the darkness of early morning, I drove to the Cathedral in Casablanca which, like other cathedrals and most other churches in Northwest Africa, is used by the American Chaplains for their services. The bishops and priests of Algeria and Morocco are most hospitable and they express great gratification at the way in which the American soldiers and sailors attend to their religious duties.

The American troops have been very helpful and generous with the missionaries. American gunfire damaged the Casablanca Cathedral and the contributions of American boys have paid for the repairs. This procedure will probably be followed on larger scales and in larger fields. We are destroying cities now, and paying dearly to do so, cities which we shall be called on later to pay to rebuild. There is a triple cost: first, the cost of the guns and munitions necessary to destroy a city; secondly, the value of the destroyed city; and thirdly, the cost of rebuilding the city. This triple payment is cheaper, however, than paying once for any damage that might have come to cities in our own land.

I made a most interesting tour of the harbor of Casablanca. We saw the havoc wrought by the battleships *Massachusetts, Brooklyn,* and *Augusta,* under the command of Admiral Hewitt. It was strange and thrilling to hear from the Admiral's lips the description of the battle in which our forces were victorious. One of the damaged vessels is the *Jean Bart,* a ship which at the time was more powerful than any in the American Navy. There are holes through her sides, fore and aft, large enough for trains to enter. Ruins of other ships half sunken, or sunken with only mastheads visible, form a grotesque monument to the power of our fire. And now the irony of it all! Americans and French are working together to clear the harbor, to salvage the ships, and to fight together.

On Friday, March 12th, I received a telegram: "You are requested to speak to the soldiers on the radio from 4 o'clock to 4:15 on Sunday. Unless we hear from you, we shall assume that everything is all right." I thought I should like to do it, but when and how to prepare for the broadcast was a question to which I did not know the answer. However, I decided to say "yes" and in some way or another get the speech ready. As at home, the only time available for such matters was after every one else went to bed. The censor was kindly present as I was writing the address, both to censure me for not having it ready sooner and to censor what I said. I told him that I did not think he would object to anything I had to say because I was following rather closely the Ten Commandments, the Declaration of Independence, and the Atlantic Charter. Just as I finished it I learned that it was a broadcast not alone to North Africa but also to the United States. I am including the speech in this letter in case you did not hear it on the radio:

Soldiers and sailors of the United States in North Africa:

Gladly do I accept this invitation to speak to you. For more than a week I have been in North Africa, visiting many places, traveling more than 2,000 miles, seeing and meeting many of you under varied conditions of military life. To me you have been an inspiration and I consider these days that I have already spent with you and the days to come that I am still to be with you among the most sacred of my life.

In these solemn circumstances when, as modern crusaders, you are working and fighting, living and dying, to preserve our nation, our ideals and our liberties, I have been thrilled beyond expression to observe the spirit of high resolve with which you are animated and the unity of purpose that is everywhere manifest among you. Your destiny is not alone to live protected under the folds of the Star-Spangled Banner and to sing in chorus its soul-stirring verses. Your vocation is something infinitely more noble and responsible, for you are writing again in imperishable glory its immortal stanzas.

"Then conquer we must when our cause it is just, and this be our motto: In God is our trust."

You are the sacred instruments of the triumph of our cause. You are the example to Americans in the homeland, not alone in the firm belief in the justice of our struggle, because we were treacherously plotted against and attacked by a combination of aggressor nations, but you are also an example to your fellow-Americans in your supreme faith in victory.

Your fellow-Americans may have some illusions in regard to what that victory will cost. But it is no illusion to you. You know full well and full seriously the cost, for part of the price of this precious victory has already been paid. It is true that all Americans both individually and collectively must bear this cost. But yours is the greater and harder portion, though those you love and those who love you bear with you something of the pain, the honor and the glory.

With you first things come first. And therefore you know how that victory must come before the fruits of victory; and those who attempt to force the ripening of the fruits or snatch them prematurely may imperil or retard victory itself. Likewise do you soldiers give us incentive in all things that are essential to the unity of our country.

We Americans are diverse in many ways and divided in many matters—and probably in too many ways and in too many matters, and frequently all to acrimoniously—but I believe that never before in our history have we Americans been more fervently united not only in love of our country but also in appreciation of it, in our faith in her destiny and in our determination to do our utmost in her service. Your unity of purpose should be a good example to all your fellow-Americans, that at home they may strive to live together with increasing mutual respect for one another and with a desire to be cooperative one with another for the common good.

Men of every racial and national origin compose the Armed Forces of the United States, and all are strongly secure in their faith in victory and united in their belief and hope in the end of that victory: the achievement of a just and lasting peace. Our war aims and our peace aims are no secret. They have been stated again and again with utmost clarity and sincerity.

On Lincoln's Birthday our President reaffirmed them and said, "In our uncompromising policy we mean no harm to the common people of the Axis nations." The President's words on that occasion were but a reaffirmation of America's undeviating attitudes and actions for the past half-century. In 1918, for example, when America had invitations to assume mandates and protectorates, America did not appropriate even a square inch of land, and long before the outbreak of the present war the independence of the sovereign Commonwealth of the Philippines was well on its way to realization.

Likewise have we engaged to respect the territorial integrity of Spain and Portugal, and also have agreed not to remain longer in French North Africa than military exigencies require. The fact that imperialism is not an American war aim or peace aim is known to our Allies, to our enemies and to all the world. We Americans ardently desire to retain our freedom, our own form of government, our right to live, to worship, to work, to assemble, to trade, to express ourselves, to defend ourselves, to live at peace with God and with our neighbors. In this sense our war aims and our peace aims are strictly defensive against alien, totalitarian world orders. But in a broader sense American war and peace aims represent the aspirations and hopes of all freedom-loving people.

The President of the United States and the Prime Minister of Great Britain have defined them and subscribed to them, and the leaders of several other peoples have also subscribed to them. These objectives are the natural rights of man and express the desires of his conscience. They echo clearly the traditional teaching of the Church, the Christian life and the Christmas allocutions of His Holiness, Pope Pius XII.

One year ago this month, President Roosevelt wrote to you soldiers and sailors of the United States, members of the American Expeditionary Forces, telling you that you bore with you the hope and confidence, the gratitude and prayers of your families, your fellow-citizens and your Commander-in-Chief. In that letter the President described America as a Godfearing, courageous people which throughout its history had put freedom under God before all purposes. And it is true that your service draws its deepest significance and its greatest strength from God, for we believe that in serving our country in her just cause, we are also serving God.

This, too, was also stated by President Roosevelt in his celebrated message on our freedoms: "Storms from abroad," the President said, "directly challenge three institutions indispensable to Americans now as always. The first is religion. It is the source of the other two, democracy and international good faith."

Religion, by teaching man his relationship to God, gives the individual a sense of his own dignity and teaches him to respect himself by respecting his neighbor. And the abandonment of the teachings and practices of religion in personal life, in social life, in civic life and in national and international life, has brought the world to the brink of chaos. The way back to peace with justice after victory is therefore in the same order. Personal righteousness, domestic integrity, social justice, civic virtue and national and international law and order.

To believe in God is not enough. We must live our lives as if we believed in Him, and not a few minutes of our lives, but all our lives. There are some who say they do not believe in God. The Old Testament and the New Testament call all men foolish who do not know of God's existence. And to all solders looking upwards to this black, star-studded African sky, the same sky into which St. Augustine gazed and from the same places in which he lived, I pray that Almighty God will give the same blessings and the same answer that He gave Augustine through the stars when to his silent questioning they answered: "We are not the God whom thou seekest—He made us."

Yes, the stars proclaim in luminous, unerasable language the existence of God, for they navigate the firmament in a certain, definite way, and the order in their movement presupposes an intelligence that cannot come from matter or from chance. And the first great Cause, Who regulates celestial orders, Who designed our bodies, resulting from the union of a hundred perfectly co-ordinated masterpieces, we know by the name of God. Every fiber of our bodies, every power of our souls, proclaims the existence of God, and to that God and Creator, our Ultimate End, we wish to be faithful and loyal.

Our Commander-in-Chief has told us that our soldiers in Tunisia are well trained and well equipped. We can be absolutely certain that they will conduct themselves bravely and effectively. Thus we are assured of victory, not only of our mighty might over our enemies, but also over the souls of their righteous people because we shall keep our national soul inviolate through our scrupulous adherence to national honor. We shall also keep our own individual souls in close union with God through our belief in Him, through repentance for our past sins because we have offended Him—Who is goodness itself— through simple prayers and acts of faith, hope, love and contrition imploring God's mercy on our souls.

Thus in time and eternity shall we be forever and ever united to Him.

After the broadcast I went to a Red Cross Club where there was a very large number of soldiers and sailors on Sunday afternoon leave. I could remain there only an hour because I was expected to visit several torpedoed ships. One of them had had everything happen to her. Torpedoed, bombed and shipwrecked, nevertheless, she successfully debarked her troops and cargo.

I continued my visits to the sick and wounded in hospitals; and conducted religious services, gave many informal talks to soldiers.

Always going places and always leaving them, always meeting people and always saying good-bye! Life is a kaleidoscope, and frankly for me over here it is a disconcerting one. So many things are new to me. It is hard for me to experience war. It is hard for me to understand war even though I know full well that America has been forced into this war; that she is engaged in it with the highest motives. As well as I can judge the American viewpoint, America is crusading even in the midst of the sordid barbarism of war. America wants all people to have true liberty, happiness, and prosperity. Now that her sons and daughters are fighting all over the world, America is more interested, yes, mightily more interested in world affairs, in world welfare, and world peace than ever before. America must know, however, that to get peace, a lasting peace, she will be obliged to do something more than say: "Let us have peace!"

Peace means tranquillity with order. It means "good will to all men." And just as buildings destroyed must be rebuilt, so, too, the fabric of man's spirit must be rewoven with threads of justice and charity. Sorrow and suffering have united many groups of people and many nations, and universal sorrow and suffering may weave a cloth of gold, in trust and understanding, in tolerance and helpfulness. Can such a thing be? I certainly hope so and pray so, and millions are doing the same.

One day I had luncheon with General Karl Spaatz, and twelve other high ranking American and British air force officers.

General Spaatz had just been named Lieutenant General and I am sure that you have read all about him. He is quiet, very matter-of-fact, and very optimistic.

It is a fascinating experience to meet many persons that we read much about in the papers and in magazines, and to meet others that I believe we shall read about in the future. I may not mention the names of all the persons I met, but I was privileged to know many of the well-known figures in the American, British, and French forces. One of these was Lieutenant-General Mark W. Clark, the Commanding General of our Fifth Army. General Clark was one of the first Americans to land in North Africa. He received me at his headquarters. Young, the youngest of his rank in our army, strikingly tall, vital, General Clark is reputedly very close to his men. I was billeted with his chief of staff, Major General Albert Greunther, distinguished mathematician and famous bridge player. In the evening I went to General Clark's home where I met many of his staff and visiting officers, among them General Moran, General Blesse and General Noce. That same day I had met General Truscott, General Harmon, and General Wilbur. Nearly all these Generals participated in the North African landings; and hearing from their own lips the story of these landings does something more to one than just reading about it. But even hearing about it from them is far short and far different from actually having been there at that moment—certainly one of the greatest moments of history, and one of the turning moments and turning places of the war.

The story of the planning and the remarkably successful carrying out of that operation would and will fill volumes. What the American correspondents have already written fills volumes.

They themselves are writing history as it has never before been written factually, accurately, and brilliantly. I am amazed when I read newspaper accounts and magazine articles. The American public is certainly well informed about what is going on over here as far as the active participation of our soldiers in the war is concerned. If people read these accounts attentively and with maps, there will be no underestimation of the tremendous and complicated task we are accomplishing with order and dispatch, and, above all, with the certainty of success.

One appreciates over here, I think, even more than one appreciates at home, the great and vitally essential contribution that the American farmer, miner, factory worker, and transport man are making to the war effort, for no diver needs a continuous flow of air through the life line more than our own men over here need a vast and a continuous flow of supplies.

But enough for the present about what I think and a little more about where I went, how I went, and what I did after I got there. Well, I did not go everywhere, but I went to many parts of everywhere—"Somewhere in North Africa." I flew in planes of many types and on various errands; sometimes with soldiers, sometimes with cargo, sometimes with the wounded. I went in autos, jeeps, peeps, and on foot. What I did after I got to a place varied with the time and with other circumstances.

When I finished dictating my last letter, I went to an airport and recited the rosary with Father Forrester's men. There were about two hundred men present for the afternoon Mass and rosary. The place is an old shed, with an earthen floor, but as Our Lord said, wherever two or three gathered in His name, there would He be in their midst, and I feel that Our Lord was very much present with us that afternoon as we participated in these religious exercises and sang several hymns.

One day at the request of the commanding officer of a regiment of Irish Guards, I distributed shamrocks for the men to wear on St. Patrick's Day. This is a custom of the Irish Guards. Incidentally, they are very proud because General Sir Harold Alexander, Deputy Commander-in-Chief of all the Allied Forces in North Africa, is an Irish Guardsman.

On St. Patrick's Day I was a passenger on a transport carrier with four officers and ten soldiers. We had a cargo of medical supplies and flew "on the deck" most of the way, which means that we just skimmed the ground. This lessens the probability of detection from planes above and prevents attacks from below. However, the Germans at this time in this particular area were not attacking isolated planes; and fighter escorts are no longer assigned to accompany the transports. The planes have various names and figures painted on them to record the number and kind of missions in which they have been used. There are, for example, small parachutes stamped on the nose to indicate each mission with para-troopers. Bombs depicted on the plane represent the number of bombing missions; red crosses show the number of trips taken with wounded; and square blocks designate missions with soldiers or cargoes brought to the front.

Late in the afternoon, I offered Mass for eight hundred American soldiers. Afterwards, as usual, I met each soldier personally. In my general talk to all the group, I told them that I was just as happy to be observing St. Patrick's Day with them in this leaky, barn-like hall, somewhere very near the front in North Africa, as I would have been in St. Patrick's Cathedral in New York. It was a large group of men to be together in this particular sector. And they were men, real men, every one of them, and I shall not forget this association with them.

Father William Walsh and Father Patrick Ryan, both regular army Chaplains from St. Paul, Minnesota, accompanied me that evening to the headquarters of the 97th Bombardment Group, where we were the guests of Colonel S. J. Donovan of Portland, Maine. General Atkinson and other officers of the Command were present to celebrate St. Patrick's Day, crowded into a room in the old farm house, which serves as Air Force headquarters. The dinner was a very special one as Colonel Donovan had located some turkeys.

We left this place about nine o'clock and drove through heavy rain and mud to the headquarters of Major General James H. Doolittle. General Doolittle really embarrassed me with his kindness, for, despite my protestation, he gave up his room to Father Walsh and me. We did not have very long to sleep, as an early Mass was scheduled for me at the 61st General Hospital. Again we rode through the darkness, the rain and the mud, to the hospital, which is staffed largely by doctors and nurses from Camden, New Jersey. Doctors, nurses, and some patients stood around in their muddy boots in the combination building that served for recreation and religious purposes, and attended the service. Chaplain T. J. Kelly of Cleveland, Ohio, assisted me.

After leaving the hospital, I visited a negro ordnance unit where I saw many soldiers from New York. Later in the morning I met the Chaplains in this area. All are reported to be distinguishing themselves in valiant service. I like to hear so many officers and men say of their own Chaplains, "He is the best Chaplain in the army!"

Recently we have had several Chaplains "missing in action." One must not give up hope at this report, for there have been some remarkable reappearances. Frequently men "missing in action" are located as prisoners. There are literally hundreds of instances of men lost for considerable periods who eventually, at times almost miraculously, succeed in getting back to their outfit. I have just heard of an American pilot who was shot down in the water and believed lost. However, he was taken prisoner by an Italian submarine. On the way back to Italy, the submarine was destroyed by the British. The pilot was again thrown into the water. This time he was rescued by a British destroyer and brought to Malta. He is now back in service on this front.

I would like to mention the names of all the Chaplains I met and tell something about the life and work of each one of them, for each one is a very individual person. For that matter, every person in and out of the armed services has a story and is a story. Some of the Chaplains are really supermen, and tragic emergencies demand supermen. Chaplains are also required to be resourceful. Father McCreedy of Philadelphia had an underground chapel which accommodated one hundred and fifty men. Father Chataignon of Galveston, Texas, was moving so fast that I think he must have had his Mass kit with him at all times, for I never caught up with him. I have mentioned Father Forrester's afternoon Mass, where I led the recitation of the rosary for two hundred soldiers and nurses. The nurses present on this occasion serve in the air transport service, evacuating the seriously wounded. This nursing service under army nurse, Miss Grogan, of St. Paul, Minnesota, has done remarkable work in saving lives that otherwise would certainly have been lost. But again, why particularize? Every one that I meet in every outfit that I visit in every service is contributing something to the cause of victory, something to the cause of peace.

Somewhere over the Mediterranean
March 19, 1943

At General Doolittle's headquarters I met General Vandenburg and Colonels Fitzpatrick, Engler, and Bartrem of his staff. These opening days of a new campaign to drive the Axis forces from Africa are exciting, and I am in a whirling cycle of emotions. Naturally I have no competency in the strategy of warfare, but being in the middle of things one gets impressions and also an occasional idea. I marvel more and more at the tremendous task of planning, producing and manufacturing everything, transporting it to North Africa, and getting it exactly where it is needed. If we only have an opportunity and a will to put such thought, energy, and help into building up the world after this war, I believe we can succeed.

The roads in North Africa are lined with long convoys and great centers for storing food, ammunition, and other supplies. The preparations for taking care of the wounded seem to be very well attended to: many evacuation hospitals, many airplanes for removing seriously injured troops, and even doctors, chaplains, and attendants are trained to parachute down to the wounded. Many things that we pride ourselves on doing well at home are done equally well over here. Many airports in Africa are busier than La Guardia Field in peace time. So, too, are many hospitals over here as busy and just as efficiently conducted, with just as high a percentage of recoveries, as are the best hospitals in America. All our officers and men are imbued with a confidence which is well founded; for the graph of our effectiveness on offense is rising and the graph of the Axis offense is in sharp decline. The graph of our morale is high, and we know that the Axis morale is declining.

General Alexander had invited me to his headquarters for luncheon, and had sent his car and Captain Clark, his aide-de-camp, for me. General Porter, of General Eisenhower's staff, also accompanied me. After luncheon, General McCreary, who is General Alexander's Chief of Staff, and Air Marshal Conyngham, brought me to the war room. The walls of the tent are covered with all kinds of maps showing the position of the various troops. Other indications, also, are given in great detail, not only those which concern us but also forces opposing us. This is the head of the operation section of the North African campaign. Naturally, reading of tragic events in the newspapers, and hearing of them every day, one inevitably and unconsciously becomes calloused and also stunned a bit into incomprehension of what is happening and of what events and figures signify in human suffering; but I freely admit that it was an emotional ordeal to stand in that tent and see the outline of the plans, hear the difficulties, and know of the consequences involved in the winning of this battle of Tunisia.

When I returned to General Doolittle's headquarters, I heard of the death, in England, of Cardinal Hinsley. While I had intended to remain longer in this particular area, still I felt that, since I intended to go to England during my trip, now would be the most appropriate time and thus I could attend the Cardinal's funeral.

I decided to leave at once, and here I am writing to you from a plane flying over the Mediterranean toward Gibraltar. The ride gives me a chance to reflect on the experiences of the past few weeks. I am thinking of battles, of consequences of battles, and of the many problems in North Africa even after the expulsion of the German and Italian armies from Tunisia. There will still be national, racial, economic, and social problems. For example, many of the Arabs live in the same way now as they have lived for hundreds of years. A walk through a native quarter of any city or town is disheartening. Many of the people want to work only just enough to gain enough to live. An ordinary sight, yet a strange one, is to see a full-grown, strong, healthy Arab standing by the side of the road, holding up one egg in his hand to sell it to some passerby for five francs, or ten cents. He will sell one egg for five francs but he will give two eggs for a box of matches. Here we are back farther in time than when the Indians sold Manhattan Island to the Dutch. General Porter told me that he could not get his laundry done for money, but he could get anything done in exchange for some article. In parts of Africa a native may not work for money, but he will work hard for two weeks for a pair of overalls.

One viewpoint of the soldiers that is stressed, but I do not think sufficiently, is that they worry more about their loved ones at home than they do about any imminence of danger here. In fact, one soldier went to the extent of saying, "My mother is the real soldier." Their desire to receive mail cannot be over-emphasized. They keep reading the letters they receive, over and over again until the ink fades and the paper wears out. Whether they be generals or privates, they have pictures of loved ones in their rooms, huts, and tents. They carry snapshots of their dear ones wherever they go. To my mind this thought of home, this remembrance, this loyalty to home and to spiritual values, is the most important foundation of the soldier's morale. He lives, he is brave and cheerful, he suffers, fights and dies for those at home and in the homeland. Occasionally, some think they "help morale" by producing vulgar shows for the soldiers. They produce "dirt" all right, but they do "dirt" in every sense of the word to the boys and the country. I was told that at a camp show Joe Brown was entertaining the men, and one soldier shouted some improper suggestion. Joe interrupted the show long enough to reprove the heckler and the crowd applauded Joe.

We are in sight of the shores of Spain and shall arrive soon in Gibraltar.

I flew from General Doolittle's headquarters in North Africa to Gibraltar in less time than it took a telegram to cover the same distance. I had wired Gibraltar asking for a reservation on a plane leaving for England. However, the non-arrival of the telegram made no difference because there were no transport planes scheduled for departure. The only available plane bound for England was a freighter filled with mail sacks, leaving at midnight. Since I did not know the day of the funeral of Cardinal Hinsley and did not wish to be late, I decided to become part of the cargo. The plane was completely and solidly packed, and I crawled into the middle of the packing. There was no possibility of communicating with the crew. There were many sacks of mail, but each mail sack had small sharp corners so that I was unable to use any one of them for a pillow. I had no overcoat or blanket, and during the long nine-hour journey, I was extremely cold and uncomfortable, for we flew at a considerable height and made our journey much longer by going out to sea. Between the cold and the corners, I could not sleep a wink. I recited my rosary; I tried to keep from freezing by moving my fingers, clasping my arms, and thinking of many hot places I had been in, to compensate for the cold. Fortunately, the trip was not rough and I was not punctured into a sieve. At long last I arrived at an airfield somewhere in England.

I went to the parish church and got myself thawed out. Later in the morning, I proceeded to London by train. Since no one knew that I was arriving at Gibraltar, I did not expect any one to know that I was arriving in London. I hoped to rest and get cleaned up; for, not only I, but also my clothes needed cleansing. However, the British Air Force Intelligence Service had sent word of my arrival and, I was surprised when I stepped off the train at Paddington Station to find a large crowd to greet me, and the largest line-up of cameras that I had ever encountered. Among those who came to meet me was Archbishop William Godfrey, the Apostolic Delegate whom I had known in Rome both when he was a student and when he was Rector of the English College. Archbishop Godfrey invited me to be his guest at the Apostolic Delegation, and I accepted his hospitality.

In starting to leave the parking place at Paddington Station, the Apostolic Delegate's car turned too sharply, hit a United States Army car parked next to it, and punctured a tire. This incident was called an accident, and I was in a "crash." Later, telegrams began to arrive, and Bishop McIntyre was among those who sent queries to the Administrator of Westminster Cathedral to learn if I had been injured. Monsignor Howlett told me he replied that I was well and that I was celebrating Mass in the Cathedral the next day, which was Sunday, March 21st. I offered this Mass in Westminster Cathedral for the repose of Cardinal Hinsley's soul.

During the morning I met General Frank M. Andrews, Commander-in-Chief of the United States forces in the European area. Instinctively one likes General Andrews. One would be puzzled to know his profession if he were not in uniform. He seems to be an "all round" man, kind, considerate, incisive. His men idolize him. They like him. They are proud of him. They know that he foresaw the war and foresaw the way in which it would be fought. I called on Mr. Freeman Matthews, Chargé d'Affaires of the American Embassy. Mr. Matthews told me that Mr. Winston Churchill had invited me to luncheon with him at the famous Number Ten Downing Street the day after the Cardinal's funeral. I asked Mr. Matthews to tell the Prime Minister that I was grateful for the invitation and that I accepted it.

Chaplain John Foley of Boise, Idaho, who is stationed in this area, accompanied me on Sunday afternoon and often thereafter on my visits to various places. The Military Attaché of the Embassy, Colonel Arthur McChrystal of San Francisco, Major John K. Cunningham of Washington, and Major Robert O'Hara went with me to the Westminster Cathedral to hear Very Reverend Robert I. Gannon, S.J., President of Fordham University, preach a sermon. Major O'Hara is a brother of Bishop O'Hara whom he resembles in speech and in features. After Father Gannon's sermon, there was an impromptu reception for the officers and enlisted men of the United States Army. That evening I called on Bishop Myers, the administrator of the diocese, and had dinner with Bishop Matthew, the other Auxiliary Bishop of Westminster.

I passed Monday visiting units conducted by the American Red Cross in London. Mr. Harvey Gibson and Mrs. S. Sloan Colt were with me on these visits. These clubs are not only well conducted, but they are well patronized by thousands of our boys. American people would be gratified to see that in London, a great "leave" center for the soldiers, everything possible is being done to make them feel at home. Of course, it is easier to do things for soldiers in a great city like London than in isolated places where many of our troops are stationed.

That evening I had dinner with Mr. Anthony Biddle, the

American Ambassador and Minister to many of the occupied countries of Europe. I met General de Gaulle at the Ambassador's home. He is the champion and the leader of a large group of his fellow-countrymen. His figure is the rallying point of a great portion of those who believe that the government of France forfeited its right to be the government when it remained in France and agreed to an armistice with Germany. The General was the French officer of highest rank who rejected the armistice, escaped to England, and continued to incite French opposition to the Nazis.

The next day, Tuesday, March 23rd, was the funeral of Cardinal Hinsley. The Delegate and I went to the Cathedral together. The ceremony was most impressive, largely attended, and one that showed appropriate honor to the great priest and the stalwart Englishman that was Cardinal Hinsley. He was already a man burdened with years and with service in Rome and in East Africa when Pope Pius XI named him to the see of Westminster. He was comparatively unknown in England because the greater part of his life had been lived abroad. Seventy years old when he became Archbishop, in less than eight years he became universally respected and beloved.

The Cardinal had requested to be buried with as little ceremony as possible, with few candles around the catafalque, and with no eulogy. However, as usually happens in such cases, popular demand prevailed over the Cardinal's own desires, and the fullest honors were given him. I was privileged to give one of the absolutions at the Cardinal's requiem. Archbishop Downing's eulogy was simple, direct, appropriate, and adequate. At the funeral I had occasion to meet many of the English bishops, who were most cordial in their greetings and generous in their expressions of appreciation of my coming to England to honor the Cardinal. By special permission of the English authorities, the body was interred in the Cathedral.

On Wednesday, I had the honor of having luncheon with the Prime Minister, Mr. Winston Churchill. It was the first luncheon at which he had any guests since his illness. Mrs. Churchill, himself, his daughter Mary, and Mr. Brendan Bracken, his former private secretary and present Minister of Information, were the only ones present.

Mr. Churchill's first question to me was, "May I without irreverence ask if you are a 'short snorter'?" As I explained to you in an earlier letter, a "short snorter" is one who has crossed the ocean in an airplane. The certificate of membership in this society consists of signatures on a dollar bill which must be always in a short snorter's possession. If the person challenged is unable to produce the certificate of his short snortership, he is penalized by being obliged to treat everyone to a short "snort," that is, a small drink. The price of the treat has now been stabilized at a dollar. Bishop O'Hara once complimented me ambiguously by saying that he had never seen anyone who could dive into a larger pile of papers and find the proper one with more luck than I could. So, too, was I fortunate on this occasion. Digging into my pockets crammed with various medical certificates, lists of persons, and letters of introduction, I produced my dollar bill which now bears the signature of men of considerable importance. Winston Churchill signed my dollar bill and I signed his; thus as members of the same club we began a most amiable conversation which lasted until three o'clock.

Everyone participated in the conversation, which naturally centered about the war and its progress. Mrs. Churchill shared in the discussion with great freedom and vivacity, her presence and that of Subaltern Mary Churchill, just home for a few days' furlough, making it a family luncheon. Brendan Bracken is a member of the household and an important one, with his reservoir of knowledge and sparkling observations.

To describe the progress of the war Mr. Churchill had some time ago coined the phrase, "the end of the beginning." The phrase was inspired by the victories of General Montgomery's Eighth Army in Egypt and Libya, the landing of General Eisenhower's forces in Morocco and Algiers, the turning of the tide of battle on the Volga and the mass airplane raids on industrial centers in Germany. These raids, in my opinion, constitute a very important "second front" in Europe, a vertical second front. If, therefore, we have passed "the end of the beginning," we are now either in the middle or at the beginning of the end. Despite prevailing optimism, realists believe that we are still in the middle of the war and not yet near the beginning of the end.

England's spirit is very high, and rightly so. Through the blackness of the night, when the inconceivable seemed inevitable, and all believed that England was about to be invaded, Mr. Churchill saw the streaks of dawn. And now it is morning in England.

It was fascinating to watch and listen to Mr. Churchill, and to reflect. His complete and brilliant mastery of the English language is just as evident in his ordinary conversation as it is in his prepared speeches. What history he has made and is making! What history he is and will be! The King's first Minister must know geography, and Mr. Churchill knows it as few men do. Mr. Churchill follows Socrates' "Know thyself." He also knows the world. He has "gone places."

The subject of religion came up. Mr. Churchill said that he is a man of faith. He believes that Almighty God has saved England in several critical situations. Notably, he remarked the failure of the Germans to follow up their success at Dunkirk, the calm sea which prevailed for the first day in many weeks at the time of the invasion of North Africa, and several other occurrences of like moment. With gratitude he spoke of the great and increasing contribution of America to the war effort, and with admiration and affection of President Roosevelt.

We discussed the rebuilding of parts of cities that had been destroyed, and the financing of these projects. I explained the plan of mutual insurance against war damage that is in effect in America, and illustrated the plan by telling Mr. Churchill that the annual premium for this type of insurance on St. Patrick's Cathedral in New York is ten thousand dollars. He offered to take the risk if I would pay him the premium. I replied that I would not risk letting him assume the risk.

The Prime Minister brought me into the cabinet room, the same room in which England declared war on the American colonies. He gave me one of the little slips that he attaches to documents requiring immediate attention. The slip, which intrigued me, is bright red; stamped in black letters upon it is: "Action This Day." That was a day of action for me. But every day, during these days over here, is a day of action for everybody. In attending to urgent matters, I have somewhat the same system as Mr. Churchill, and I hope that when I return to New York I shall find my desk and various trays as empty as they were on February 9th when I told all those with whom I work to "carry on."

That afternoon I met many of the Chaplains of the famous

Eighth Air Force. I spoke to them as a group and afterwards talked with them individually. Nothing in my trip gives me greater pleasure than these informal visits with the Chaplains— the fulfillment of the purpose of my journey. I was to meet these men later at their various posts of duty, but this general reception gave all of us the opportunity to be together. It reminded me of the monthly gatherings of the Chaplains at the school in Harvard University.

In the afternoon I met Bishop Dey, Military Vicar of the British Army, Father Coughlin, principal Catholic Chaplain in the British Army, and Father O'Neil, Chief Chaplain of the Canadian forces. That evening I had dinner with Brendan Bracken in his apartment in the building of the British War Information Service. Those present included the Apostolic Delegate, Archbishop Godfrey, and the Duke of Norfolk.

Among the many old friends I saw in London was John McCormack. John is growing old a bit more rapidly than some of us. I had seen him only once since the great day ten years ago when he sang Panis Angelicus during the Pontifical Mass at the close of the Eucharistic Congress in Dublin. There were flashes of the old fire in the eyes of the man who, year after year and day after day, filled the concert halls of Great Britain, America, and Australia. During the hour we had together, I let my mind fade back from the John of today to that jaunty, confident figure of years before whose voice and warmth of spirit made him universally beloved.

One afternoon, I called on Sister Gregory, of the Little Company of Mary Nursing Sisters, whom I had not seen since I was sick in the hospital in Rome twenty-nine years ago. In the meantime she was assigned to duty in South Africa where she labored for many years. Now she is stationed in a convalescent home, some thirty miles outside of London. She looks very well, and we had a most enjoyable time talking of the years when I was a student in the American College. I told her that I still have, in Whitman, the alb that the Sisters at the hospital gave me to use when I was ordained a priest.

As I have already said, the spirit of the people in London is very good. There are many reasons for this, but the great reason is that the feeling of victory is in the air and in the blood. Air raids are infrequent now and of no military consequence. The city is calm, peaceful, and safe. The ninety-two successive days of raids against the practically unprotected city seem long ago. One still sees the ruins, the concrete piles for anti-tank defenses, and obstacles in fields to prevent the landing of hostile planes. However, the street signs have been restored. A person can always know in which direction London is because the cross bars on poles supporting telephone wires are affixed to the pole on the side nearer to London.

One of the many highlights of my visit to England was the time I spent with the Eighth Air Force commanded by General Ira C. Eaker. The General is the father of this Air Force, one of the first generals to demonstrate the practicability of precision bombing in daytime. His manner is quiet but convincing as he evaluates the contribution of air power to victory. He uses graphs and photographs to show in the simplest, most effective manner the problems ahead and their solution. He was most cordial, hospitable, and kind, and arranged for me to visit all the military installations in his command. He himself gave me much time, and I met many of his officers and men, including General Ansell, General Longfellow, Colonel Creighton, and Major O'Hara.

I managed to see nearly all the Chaplains stationed in England. I took a long trip by automobile to a place inaccessible by air, to visit Father W. A. Irwin, of Philadelphia, who was seriously ill in a hospital. His first words well repaid me for the journey. "I was wondering," he said, "if you could get up here to see me." *

My tour brought me to many parts of England that I had known in happier days. I went to Oxford, Stratford-on-Avon, Coventry, and Bristol. These last two towns have suffered greatly. The ruins of Coventry Cathedral are tragic in themselves and in their significance.

Now that the Allies have the preponderance of air power, there may be retribution and retaliation. If we could keep the spirit of revenge out of our action, if we could continue to concentrate our operations on military objectives, if we could punish the guilty responsible leaders who have brought disaster on their own peoples and on us, we should have an easier task of reconstruction after the war. But if we use Nazi tactics in their full malice with the full power that we are mustering by indiscriminately obliterating everything in every city, we are bound to suffer ourselves. This is my conviction. Let us win the war without destroying our victory.

The days in England were full, and went all too quickly. I met General Hartle on several occasions and he was very helpful in arranging matters for me to visit troops in many areas.

One afternoon, I visited a division composed mostly of Maryland, Virginia, and New England troops, under command of General Gerow. In the neighborhood there is one of the finest Red Cross Clubs that I have ever seen. It occupies a great and magnificent mansion surrounded by acres of beautiful grounds.

* Father Irwin has since died.—Editor.

The director is Mrs. Roosevelt, whose husband, General Theodore Roosevelt, is in Africa. Although her husband, sons, and son-in-law were in the service, she said that she could not be happy without making the contribution of herself to the war effort overseas. She had just received the consoling news that her son Quentin was recovering from serious injuries received in air combat in North Africa.

After this tour of military installations I returned to the Apostolic Delegation. So that I might have longer visits with some friends, Archbishop Godfrey invited them to luncheon and dinner. One of these was General Sikorsky * that great figure of Poland, and great figure of the war. He remained for an hour after luncheon talking of his stricken but brave people. General Sikorsky is more than Poland's Prime Minister. He is Poland. His people, his soldiers, his exiles, his country, place their faith in him. He will never betray them. As you know, when he was in New York a short time ago, he was present at Mass in the sanctuary of St. Patrick's Cathedral on the Sunday morning of his departure for England. The New York people had already helped Poland, but I had received some donations for charity and it did my heart good to be able to give General Sikorsky a check for ten thousand dollars for his suffering countrymen. Poland's misery is so great that this amount is only a little; but there was good will in the gift, which the General felt.

There are many appeals for help. In God's name and in the name of all who repose trust in me, I strive to answer all. Thus, when Prince Felix and his son Prince Jean came to luncheon at the Delegation, I took the opportunity to help Luxembourg. Since I last saw him in New York only two years ago, Prince

* Killed in airplane crash.

Jean has grown from boyhood to manhood. He is now a student at Sandhurst, the famous English Military Academy, and shortly will be commissioned an officer in the "Irish Guards."

Through Mr. Anthony Biddle, our accredited representative to Belgium, Czecho-Slovakia, Greece, Jugoslavia, the Netherlands, and Norway, I was able to help the distressed people of those countries. Every single act of interest on the part of any citizen of the United States in the welfare of the inhabitants of those invaded lands is doubly appreciated at this time of their agony. Through Bishop Myers I was enabled to help the British war sufferers; and through the *Stars and Stripes,* the newspaper published by the American soldiers, I contributed to the welfare fund of the British War Orphans.

I tried to see as many people as wished to see me, and some mornings in the Delegation reminded me of my New York days. It is impossible to see as many persons in a morning over here as I could during a morning at home because all whom I see here have more than personal problems burdening them. As in America, so over here, people appeal to me to do things that are utterly beyond my powers. I feel just as intensely myself, as does the person who is urging me to do something that just cannot be done. The extreme in this category of demands is represented by those who ask me why the Pope does not stop the war!

I had read so much about Admiral Stark, and had seen so many of his pictures that meeting him was like resuming an old acquaintance. His conspicuous and oft-remarked white hair, instead of accenting age, actually serves as a backdrop emphasizing the youthfulness of his face. One member of Parliament who came to see me was Miss Rathbone, who has been so prominent in bringing to the attention of the world the piteous plight of the Jewish people in Nazi-dominated lands. The demonstrated cruelties perpetrated on these helpless victims of racial persecution are something beyond the bounds of credibility, and rightly have aroused the indignation of the civilized world. Monsignor Shramec, the Prime Minister of Czecho-Slovakia, came to see me and told of the conditions in his unhappy land.

I had two long talks with General Charles de Gaulle. He represents the soul of France to millions of Frenchmen both inside and outside the motherland. We discussed the tragedy of France, a great nation with a great soul. Down through the centuries, her contributions to western civilization are incalculable. France has her faults and her failings; so have all nations. America owes much to France for her colonization, her protection, for the gift of her blood. Affection and gratitude toward France are early implanted in the American heart, and her present plight cannot but evoke deepest sympathy in the hearts of us all. It will be the taking of a long step forward when General de Gaulle and General Giraud are able to unite their forces, for they are both sincere patriots, leaders of great groups of suffering Frenchmen, who repose faith and hope in them.

I am now bringing my stay in England to a close. I am going to visit Ireland, and shall return to London for a few days before going back to North Africa. The last thing I did in London was to visit Bishop Amigo, the Bishop of Southwark. As New York City has two dioceses, New York and Brooklyn; London has three; Westminster, Southwark, and Brentwood. The life work of Bishop Amigo was the building of St. George's Cathedral. This cathedral has been completely destroyed and it was heart-sickening to stand with him and look at the ruins, realizing his tragedy.

There is much to think over here. Some of these thoughts I expressed in my broadcast from London. I wished you and all those at home to know that I was thinking of you, for I began my broadcast with these words:

"Where'er I roam, whatever realms to see,
My heart untravelled fondly turns to thee."

Wherever I roam, I see America and Americans, striving, struggling, suffering and dying, destroying lives to save lives, all with the intent and hope of serving our country and of saving civilization. Our goal is our own salvation, both national and personal: national in time and personal both in time and eternity, for a nation's life does not survive time and a person's salvation touches both time and eternity.

Wherever I go I ask myself if there is anything with which we may successfully oppose the hatred that has been unleashed against God and against humanity. I ask myself if we are doing everything possible to stop the march of the soldier-slaves of Cain, incarnate again. So far as I know, there is only one antonym to hate and that is love. There is one antonym to greed and that is charity. Even amid the blackness of war, there must be the light of love and charity; otherwise we shall lose not only our lives but also the war even in the winning of it. One young pilot said to me, "I don't mind losing my life, but I don't want to lose it for nothing."

As a priest I preach and strive to practice charity, and as an American I strive to be realistic in my idealism. Wars may perhaps be won by force of arms but peace is won only by justice.

Justice is the mind of civilization and charity is its heart. If America, as we know it and love it, is to win the peace as well as the war, she must be true and just to herself and to her sons and daughters, as they are proving their loyal devotion to her on all the battlefronts of the world.

The men over here are calm, determined, and sure about winning this war. No sacrifice seems too great to them if they can hope to resume the life they love, in the country they love, after the war. The contributions of the lives of these men, our brothers, will be in vain, a mockery and a crime, unless we win both the war and the peace. We shall win the war by man, brain, arms, and supply power. To win the peace we need the same powers plus the powers of the soul. The source and resource of all the powers of the soul is charity.

Charity is founded on mankind's unity in origin, nature, and destiny. It knows no boundaries of race. It is love of God and love of fellow-man in action. Charity is the foundation of justice, and justice the foundation of peace.

I had received many invitations to visit Ireland. The first one came from David Gray, the United States Minister to Eire. We knew each other in the States. I was pleased to accept his gracious hospitality and so informed him. Colonel McChrystal, the Military Attaché of the American Embassy, had business in Ireland and we went along together. Because Eire is neutral country, Colonel McChrystal dressed in civilian clothes and we left the airport at about three o'clock. We had an extremely rough trip and instead of making Dublin in one hop we were obliged to land at Liverpool for refueling. It took us over four hours to do four hundred miles. When we finally succeeded in landing in Dublin I thought that the wind would sweep us off the ground again.

At the airport I was met by the American Minister, Mr. Gray, the Secretary to the Nuncio, Monsignor Enrici, the Vice Premier, Sean O'Kelly, the Minister of External Affairs, Joseph Walshe, General Aiken and Archbishop McQuaid's secretary. All of them I had known before and it was pleasant seeing them again. Mr. Gray brought me to the American Legation in Phoenix Park, which I remembered from my visit there to see Cardinal Hayes when he was in Ireland in 1932 for the Eucharistic Congress.

Since the plane was very late, I arrived only just in time for dinner. Mrs. Gray greeted all the guests but she did not remain with us. The Prime Minister, Eamon de Valera, was present and also Archbishop McQuaid of Dublin. Other guests were the Vice Prime Minister, Sean O'Kelly, the Canadian High Commissioner, John O'Kearney, the United Kingdom Representative, Sir John Maffey, Monsignor Enrici and Colonel McChrystal. Sir John Maffey, a veteran of the British Colonial Service, told me many things that will be helpful to me on my journey. Remembering my visit to Dublin on the occasion of the Eucharistic Congress, and recalling vividly the faith of the people of Ireland, I expressed the desire to say Mass in three parish churches in different localities of the city. Archbishop McQuaid graciously arranged these matters for me.

The first Mass was at the Cathedral on Wednesday, March 31st. The church was crowded, and afterwards I spoke a few words to the congregation. Many of the people remained until I left the Church to go to the Legation, and I feared that some persons might be injured as they crowded around my car. I made a brief call on Archbishop Robinson, the Papal Nuncio. He lives in Phoenix Park not far from the American Embassy. Archbishop Pascal Robinson is an American citizen. He belongs to the Franciscan Order and for several years was stationed at St. Bonaventure's College in Alleghany, New York; afterwards he was professor in the Catholic University in Washington. Later he went to Rome where I first knew him. Before being appointed to Dublin as Nuncio, Archbishop Robinson was Apostolic Visitor in Malta and the Holy Land.

My visit to Premier De Valera lasted well over an hour. Mr. De Valera is not so thin as he was when last I saw him. He still has the appearance and the spirit of the ascetic which he is, and the manners of the professor which he was before he entered public life. In private conversation he is quiet in speech and calm in manner. He was born in New York City, and he told me that he once attended a public dinner in New York City at which he was the only born New Yorker. He is a very methodical man, evidently accustomed to doing many things himself which many men in similar positions would assign to others. On his desk he has a miniature telephone exchange, which he operates himself. His office is moderate in size and so is his desk, which was very neatly arranged.

Although she is not a belligerent, Southern Ireland has suffered from the war. Many people who criticize her because she is not actively on the Allied side do not perhaps know that there are an estimated one hundred and fifty thousand volunteers from Eire fighting in the British Army.

In the afternoon I went to see Archbishop John McQuaid. He is the lately appointed, very young Archbishop of Dublin. He is quiet in manner but like everyone whom I met in Ireland, was most heartily cordial. He accompanied me to the famous Seminary of Maynooth, the Foreign Mission Seminary of the Vincentian Fathers, and to his own Diocesan Seminary, the rector of which is Canon Dargan, a classmate of mine in Rome. In all the seminaries I gave brief talks, asked for a holiday for the students and made a gift to the rectors so that the students might enjoy the holiday. I also visited numerous churches, many of them new ones, and all in all I had a most pleasant association with Archbishop McQuaid.

That evening a dinner was given by Premier de Valera at which the Archbishop, the Auxiliary Bishop, the American Minister, the Vice Premier, the Secretary for Foreign Affairs, and several members of the Cabinet, and leaders of the various parties in Ireland were present. The dinner was held at 80 St. Stephens

Green, which is the formal residence of the Prime Minister. Mr. de Valera made a short address of welcome to me, and I responded telling of my happiness in being with them.

There have been many reasons given for my trip to Europe, but Mr. Gray was the only one, thus far, who said that I was here for a rest! After he had conducted me around or followed me around to various places for forty-eight hours, he decided that he was the one who needed the rest, so during the remainder of my visit, with the exception of my call on the President of Eire, Mr. Douglas Hyde, Mr. Gray did not accompany me. However, we went together to a luncheon at the Apostolic Nunciature and to dinner at the Archbishop's house. I called on Mr. Cosgrave at his home and met Mrs. Cosgrave and their sons. I also called on the Lord Mayor of Dublin.

For me, the visits that I made to the parish churches for the morning Masses were most consoling occasions. In no place in the world that I know of do the people in such numbers regularly attend morning Mass. And they do not have automobiles to bring them. They walk long distances even in the rain. They are people poor in this world's goods but their treasure in heaven must be very great indeed.

Ireland is very short of coal and manufactured goods, and there are acute shortages in many materials. Fortunately for Ireland, she has her peat bogs; and great piles of peat are stacked in Phoenix Park to be used, as occasion demands, for fuel purposes.

For memory's sake, I went to the place in Phoenix Park where the great altar was built for the Eucharistic Congress celebration; and I thought of the day when a million people were present on this lawn before the altar. Never before or since have

I seen that number of people gathered in one spot. It was unforgettable.

At that time I was secretary to the Papal Legate, Cardinal
Lauri; and well do I remember with what emotion I reflected
upon the contrast between the most hospitable manner in which
I was received in Ireland and the miserable way in which my
two great-grandmothers and my grandparents left their homeland, impoverished and famished, herded like cattle, packed
into the hull of a sailing vessel, and brought to America, land of
opportunity, to which they gave every ounce of their strength
and all their hearts' gratitude and devotion. From America they
received everything in return; opportunities to worship God, to
work, to make homes and to bring up children, teaching them
love of God and country and obedience to God's Commandments and our country's laws.

When it came time to leave southern Ireland, Mr. Gray said
that he would enjoy the ride to Armagh, in the north of Ireland,
where I was going to have luncheon and a visit with Cardinal
MacRory. Mr. Gray kindly took me on this three-hour journey.
Ireland is a small country, but the differences between the north
and south of Ireland are vast and deep and sad.

Cardinal MacRory, now over eighty years old, has suffered
many affronts and injustices during his lifetime, in his own
person and in the flock he shepherds. He is the successor to St.
Patrick in the see of Armagh. His Eminence is not a large man
but he is strong, well-built, erect, and active, and no man I have
ever met carries his eighty years more firmly. I once had the
honor of having His Eminence as my guest in Newton Center,
Massachusetts, when he visited America in 1934, on his return
from Australia whither he had gone as legate of the Pope. Then,

too, I had visited him when I was Cardinal Lauri's secretary in 1932. His Eminence reproved me for not remaining longer with him in Armagh but I am becoming accustomed to reproofs of this kind. They are preferable, however, to hints that I am not moving along rapidly enough.

I went with the Cardinal into St. Patrick's beautiful cathedral, and prayed for Ireland and the Irish. I thought and prayed, also, for the flock in New York who love and worship God in another beautiful cathedral that bears the name of Patrick. Together we walked outside around the cathedral and stood on the hillside. Together we looked across the valley to the opposite hill where stands a greater and more beautiful cathedral that once was Patrick's and of Patrick's faith, when faith was one in Ireland.

The Cardinal had invited all the Bishops of Northern Ireland to luncheon; they gave me an Irish welcome. I was particularly glad to meet Bishop Farren, the Bishop of Derry, who is the Vicar Delegate of the United States Forces in Northern Ireland, and has been very interested in the spiritual welfare of our troops. He is a young, zealous, intelligent, and alert-appearing bishop.

The day was Friday, April 2nd, and Cardinal MacRory had been extremely fortunate to secure a fish for the dinner. It was a very large fish and it reminded me of one I had seen mounted on a board in the office of a friend in the States. When some newspaper men asked me a great many questions which no human being could successfully and helpfully answer, I respectfully declined the opportunity either to be quoted or misquoted. When they still pressed me, I pointed to the fish on the platter and smilingly told them of the mounted fish back home with its significant label which reads: "If I had kept my mouth shut, I wouldn't be here."

The Governor of Northern Ireland, the Duke of Abercorn, had most courteously welcomed me, and I called to see him in his great mansion in Hillsborough, not far from Belfast. The Duke has been governor for twenty-two years. I remained with him only a quarter of an hour, for I was obliged to keep an engagement at General Edward Hills' headquarters. He is commanding the American forces in Northern Ireland. It was tea time when I arrived. A large number of English and American officers were present, and also members of the government. Among them was Rt. Hon. J. M. Andrews, Prime Minister. I asked him if he had ever met Bishop Farren. Since he had not met him, I introduced them to each other.

General Hill asked me to speak to the officers, soldiers, nurses, and civilian aircraft employees, from the terrace of his headquarters, and I was pleased to do so. The group was so large that I could not, to my regret, have the pleasure of greeting each one individually.

The airplane departure was scheduled to insure arrival in London before blackout time, so I was obliged to leave. General Hill brought me to the airport, and in a few minutes we were on our way back to London.

The trip south was perfect. We made the four hundred miles in two hours and a half. We flew low over the Isle of Man and passed over a convoy. We were back in the Apostolic Delegation in time for supper. Thus ended my visit to Ireland, to me a beautiful and beloved country but still a most "distressful" one.

My time in England was drawing to a close, but there were

yet many things to do. One of the most pleasant things was dinner with General Frank M. Andrews on Saturday evening, April 3rd. He had invited the Apostolic Delegate and the following generals whom I had already met and to whom I was now to say farewell—Generals John C. H. Lee, William Lee, William Key, Ingles, Longfellow, Barth, and Noce. Admiral Stark and Admiral Kaufman also were present.

Archbishop Godfrey, the Apostolic Delegate, is an Englishman. One of the generals asked him if he had ever been in America. He answered, "No." "I thought you had," said the general, "for you speak English so well." When I heard this, I told the story of an incident that occurred after I had preached a sermon during an Atlantic crossing. Two New Yorkers met me afterwards on the deck and stopped me, saying, "That was a good sermon, Father. You speak English with hardly any accent!" I replied, "Thank you too much, kind gentlemen!"

On Sunday morning, April 4th, I offered Mass for a group of service men in London. Some of the men are regularly stationed in London; others were in the city on leave. Afterwards I drove to Broadwood Cemetery where American boys of the last war are buried and also where there are graves of the casualties in this war, English, American, Canadian, Polish, Belgian, and some of other nationalities. On occasions like this, when alone, I walk from grave to grave, I understand better the meaning of war than I do when I read statistics of losses.

I returned to London in time to make a broadcast to the States, which I assume you heard and hope you enjoyed.

Monday, April 5th, was my last day in England, and it was a busy one. There were still some airfields that I had not visited; and Generals Eaker, Longfellow and Armstrong arranged for me to visit them. I arrived at one of the fields just as preparations for a bombing mission were being made. This is always a tense period. I celebrated Mass, gave absolution, and distributed Communion to a large number of these men going on this mission. I knew and the men knew that for some of them, it was their last Communion. I went with them to their airplanes, and chatted with them. It was soon time to leave. I went to the control tower and watched and counted the planes as they took off at intervals of thirty seconds. I knew the city very well that was to be the target that day and had acquaintances there. Then came the interval of waiting for the return of the planes. It seemed interminable. Finally they started coming back. One, two, three, and so on I counted, but I couldn't count them all, "back home." I went to the ground crews of the planes that were missing. There was little to say but much to feel. Once again, statistics; but I broke down statistics to individuals. I thought of the boys who didn't come back and of their families; of the great responsibility of the country and of the living to those who had given, and smilingly given, their all to America and to us.

I hurried back to London and had a farewell visit with that great man who is General Andrews, and took some personal messages from him to some friends of his in North Africa. Mr. John G. Winant, our Ambassador to Great Britain, had just returned from America that afternoon and we had half an hour together. He looked very well, and told me news of America, the President, and of mutual friends in New Hampshire, his home State, and in Washington. I had ten minutes to pack my two bags and get to the home of Ambassador and Mrs. Biddle for dinner. Mr. Churchill's private secretary, Lord Morton, Mr. Brendan Bracken, and Archbishop Godfrey were there for my last dinner in London. Having said good-bye I took the express train for Edinburgh. Train travel is not what it was before the war; and the blacked-out stations and the grimy appearance of everything are in sharp contrast with pre-war light and cleanliness. Taking the railroad, I was in Scotland "tomorrow." It was my first visit to Edinburgh. I did not know where the cathedral was, and neither did the first two people that I asked to direct me but I finally located it.

In mid-morning I went to call on Archbishop MacDonald and spent the day with him. At luncheon General Sir Maxwell Scott, a descendant of Sir Walter Scott, and the present owner of Abbottsford, invited me down to the castle; but, with the schedule for the next three days definitely fixed, I was unable to accept. After dinner I met the Lord Provost, who corresponds to our Mayor, Lord Cormont, a judge of the high court of Scotland, Chaplain Foley of Boise, Idaho, and Chaplain Boyle of New York. Together we went to see places of interest in Edinburgh, including Edinburgh Castle and the church of St. Giles, with its chapel of the Knights of the Thistle. I enjoyed the few hours we spent in sightseeing, especially my visit to St. Margaret's in the Edinburgh Castle where there is a chapel dedicated to the heroines of the last war. The chapel and its inscriptions apply with equal appropriateness and sublimity to this war, twenty-five years after, for, of the new generation may it truly be written: "In honor of all Scotch women who, amid the stress of war, sought by their labors, sympathy, and prayers to obtain for their country the blessings of peace."

In the late afternoon, we set out by motor for Glasgow where I was the guest of Canon Mullin in St. Peter's Parish. One of the first calls I made the next day was to pay my respects to

Archbishop MacIntosh. Because of his illness my visit with him was brief. Colonel Eversberg had kindly invited me to meet his officers at luncheon that day, and afterwards he arranged for me to talk with many of his men in their barracks.

I celebrated Mass the next morning at St. Peter's Church and visited the Glasgow Cathedral. Later, after buying three tartan scarfs and learning that red and bright colors are for night wear and green and dull shades are for day wear, we went to see both Loch Lomond and Ben Lomond. We drove along to —— and visited Kilmarnock and Ayr, which is the birthplace of Bobby Burns. At the airport, the chaplains and I had supper with Colonel Palmer, the Commanding Officer of the Post, and I am now writing this letter to you while waiting for the plane to take me back to North Africa!

We did not get started until midnight and it was a pleasant surprise to find real seats in the plane. It was a long flight from Scotland to North Africa. Mr. Pendar, the American Consul, met me and took me to his home, where we had a pleasant afternoon and evening together.

After saying Mass for a number of American soldiers Thursday morning, I took the plane east. It was my fifth trip across North Africa. At Oran a chaplain helped to transfer my baggage to another plane that was leaving in seven minutes for our North African Headquarters. It was late Friday afternoon when I arrived. Father Walsh requested that I officiate at the Stations of the Cross in St. Charles Church. I gave the sermon and Benediction of the Blessed Sacrament and met and talked with several hundred of the soldiers.

Sunday, I said Mass in the open air at the Headquarters of the United States fleet in the Mediterranean waters. At this service and as usual, I preached a brief sermon; then met all the officers and men personally and took their names and home addresses so that I may write to their nearest of kin when it is possible to do so.

At luncheon, I was the guest of Mr. Harold Macmillan, the British High Commissioner in North Africa; and in the afternoon I had an interesting hour with General Bedell Smith, General Eisenhower's Chief of Staff. Admiral Hewitt, the Commander-in-Chief of our fleet in African waters, and Lord Rennel of Rodd were guests that evening at the home of my host, Mr. Robert Murphy. We were fascinated by Admiral Hewitt's discussion of the Navy's part in the planning and preparation for the North African campaign as well as the details of the landing. I was fortunate to meet Lord Rennel of Rodd as he was able to give me very precise information and helpful advice concerning my trip to South Africa. In reference to this visit to South Africa, which I had not anticipated before leaving America, the British military authorities gave me the following message from Mr. Winston Churchill: "Every good wish in your work and on your travels. I am telegraphing to Field Marshal Smuts to assist you in every way."

Early Monday morning, April 12th, I began an all-day trip by plane which was very heavily loaded with men and materials. There were only two other civilian passengers, Mr. and Mrs. Charles Sulzberger. The pilot was Lieutenant Aldrich. Sergeant Rinaldi, the engineer, had just received word that he was the father of a boy and he wished to wire Mrs. Rinaldi, of New York, not to have the baby baptized until I arrived home. I could think of several reasons against this delay, so I trust that the little Rinaldi boy has been baptized by now. This is the second opportunity I have had to baptize a baby, for a family named Spellman in Armagh, Ireland, did me the honor to call their new baby by my name.

We made a stop at the Constantine Airport. The weather had changed greatly during the three weeks since I had been there. Instead of rain and mud there was now dryness and dust. This time we were on our way to Tripoli, but did not take a direct route. We flew south from Constantine over Biskra and the Sahara Desert, then to the southeast where we crossed over into

Tripoli near Nalut and started northeast for the city of Tripoli. The airport is named for Mussolini and is known as Castel Benito. It is only a little more than two months now since the Italians were driven out of Tripoli, after having been there since 1911, and after having spent lives and fortunes in the development of this city and its coastline territory. When the Italians left Tripoli, the garrison was commanded by General Bastico. By the strange coincidence I saw General Bastico, at a distance, when I was in Rome only five weeks ago. When the Italians left Tripoli on their retreat toward Tunis, they assured the population, "We will be back." They were right. They have been coming back by the thousands.

Yesterday I saw twenty thousand of them, Italian prisoners, and several thousand German prisoners herded together in a barbed wire enclosure not far from the city. Long lines of trucks filled with prisoners are still streaming through to prisoner stockades. I talked to these men at the request of the American officers. They were glad to hear someone speaking Italian. A general suggested I ask them how they liked their food. We all imagined that after the rations which they had been receiving as retreating soldiers under combat pressure, they would find the "prisoner-of-war-ration" most satisfying. Instead, they smiled and gave the "boarding-school" answer that the rations were all right but they could eat ·more! These prisoners were working at digging holes like shallow cellars, over which tents are placed to serve as hospital wards. They urged me to request the general to grant them the privilege of continuing to work, as confinement in a prison stockade, without anything to do, is very demoralizing.

These hospital wards are ingeniously made because the cellars are three feet deep and the tents placed above them give more air space and also more working space. The patients are likewise protected because the beds are below the level of the ground, and thus the danger of injuries from the explosion of enemy personnel bombs is diminished. I have already told you of the wonderful system of air evacuation of the wounded. Serious cases, especially those with head or abdominal injuries, are evacuated to fully equipped, superbly manned base hospitals.

From dressing stations that are actually under fire, the wounded are brought in ambulances to field hospitals, which are as close to the front as is possible without being within shell range. In these field hospitals, which are in tents prominently marked with red crosses, emergency surgery such as the setting of bones is done. Out of one hundred wounded who survive to be brought to field hospitals, approximately ninety-nine lives are saved! This achievement is due to the bravery of the men in the medical corps, the skill of the surgeons and nurses, and the use of sulfa drugs and blood plasma. Here again I saw evidences in lives saved by the vital contribution of men and women on the home front who have responded so generously to appeals for donations of blood.

At the Castel Benito Airport I was met by General Auby C. Strickland, Commanding General of the Ninth United States Fighter Command, and General Lush, the British Administrator of Civil Affairs of that area. General Strickland invited me to stay with him at his quarters, and I was most happy to accept. He lives in the former home of General Graziani, and General Lush, in the house in which General Balbo resided.

We all went to call on General Robertson, Commanding General of Tripoli. He is a son of General Robertson of the last war. From his office one gets a full view of the harbor of Tripoli. Like Casablanca, it is a sorry sight with sunken, half-sunken, and damaged ships of all types. A convoy had just come to Tripoli. Sfax had been taken only twenty-four hours before, but its harbor was not yet in use, and Tripoli was still the base for supplying men and materials to General Montgomery.

After his brilliant successes in El Alamein along the Egyptian coast and in Libya, General Montgomery reached Sousse yesterday on his way to Tunis. The achievements of the famous Eighth Army and Montgomery are already legendary. But they are also very actual. He does not move until he is fully prepared to move and certain of success. When his army starts, it is an irresistible moving wall. He says quite openly what he is going to do, and then does it. His forces are coordinated with the Ninth United States Air Force, under command of Major General Lewis H. Brereton.

I mentioned that a convoy had arrived in Tripoli harbor that morning. In all probability that meant an air raid that night. General Strickland said that when the raid came, we would go outside the city along the waterfront to see it. After supper I went down to the Cathedral to arrange for Mass the next morning. I had just returned when the warning sounded. General Strickland met me at the door. We got into his automobile and started away to watch the raid.

Suddenly the sky became streaked with powerful searchlights sweeping across the darkness. Anti-aircraft fire began immediately. Our planes were already in the air, for the raid was predictable. Even if it were not, they would be on patrol. In comparison with other raids this one was insignificant. There were only fifteen enemy planes involved in the attack. At them were thrown a hundred tons of anti-aircraft fire. But there is nothing that is insignificant to me. I have seen the victims of the rain of fire and steel, and I have seen war's devastation. I have also been gripped with anguish as I tried to keep on counting returning planes that did not come. War is a contagious disease. I do hope that America and Americans will have enough spirit to win the war, and enough of the spiritual not to contract the disease of war.

I remember so well the words of a man high in our government spoken three months after Pearl Harbor. He deplored the use of the word "destroy" by the Japanese and Nazis. For the Japanese were winning battles and "destroying" us. I hope that we shall be content to win battles and win the war and not over-win it. To me both self-interest and generosity prompt this philosophy; for our "unconditional surrender" terms, I think, mean that we shall make conditions for our fullest and longest protection, without driving to desperation those among our enemies who liked America and Americans in the past, and are just as much opposed to fighting us as we were reluctant to fight them.

Some phrases of the Atlantic Charter, some phrases from the addresses of its two signers, are meant to give hope to all the world. And they hit the center of the target—world peace. Our President said, "We wish no harm to the common people of the Axis nations, but we do intend to punish their guilty leaders." The common people, the common leaders, the common soldiers, both officers and men, wish to remove the decay in national lives; but I do not think that they wish the destruction of nations beyond necessity. Even selfishly it would be ruinous because it would destroy American lives and American life. The rest of us common people whose contribution to the war effort must be spiritual and moral must pray that in cutting out the cancer of Nazi and Fascist tyranny, and all other tyranny, we get all the roots of the cancer and not destroy humanity in the process. Therefore I hope in this terrible war, the leaders on our side and we, their followers, marching together, enduring together, winning together, may gain peace for the world, and gain it with some permanence so that there will be no more waste of life, substance, food and money, which means inevitably the waste of souls and bodies of men.

But I am forgetting—or am I?—that I am watching an air raid. Now a searchlight picks up a plane. The plane tries to evade. Other lights streak him. He is caught. Shells burst above, below, before, behind—all around the plane! The plane is hit. Sparks trail behind. The plane begins to fall, at first, gradually, and then the final plunge. The raid is soon over, and the General and I go back to town.

After Mass the next morning, I called on the Bishop of Tripoli, Monsignor Frassinetti. He is a Franciscan from Milan who has been in North and South America. He is an Italian citizen but, very properly, he recognizes the authority of the occupying military government. He came to see me at the invitation of General Lush, and I also went to see him. Naturally he is sad at the devastation wrought in Tripoli. His Cathedral is damaged but not seriously; every window has been broken. I visited the institute of the Franciscan Missionaries of Mary. Their beautiful chapel is completely wrecked and the school and the charity home are also considerably damaged. I met the Mother Superior and all the other Sisters. I thought them to be very calm and heroic under the circumstances. They still keep the school going but the orphans have been moved outside of Tripoli. However, they did have one waif that had been left that morning at the door of the convent by some unidentified person.

During my stay in this area, I said Mass for the 315th Service Group. There were several hundred officers and men present. The Mass was out of doors in a poppy-splashed field, so reminiscent of the last war. Colonel Cunyas is the Commanding Officer and Father Edward Farley, of Brooklyn, is the Chaplain of this unit. This organization has been most resourceful in its adaptation of the materials abandoned by the Germans and the Italians. It is a mobile unit and takes care of itself as well as the forward units that depend on it for everything.

I am going to interrupt my visit to the Tripoli sector to go to Malta. After my return to Tripoli I shall move on to the Gabes and Sfax areas of Tunisia, and possibly by that time be able to get to Sousse.

We flew to Malta in a small Lockheed plane, manned by boys from Ontario and Alberta in Canada, and from Sydney, Australia. I thought of the vastness of the British Empire as we flew east over the land as far as Homs and then started north over the Mediterranean for Malta. The trip is supposed to take only about one hour and forty minutes; when two hours passed, I began to wonder if we were going to be able to find Malta. I was sitting in the very nose of the plane and there was a compass before me. We came into Malta flying ten minutes to the south. It is well that we turned around, for in another fifteen or twenty minutes we would have been over Sicily and this would definitely have been a premature visit. Sicily is only sixty miles north of Malta.

Malta has always stood for something good in history and in courage. The knights of St. John of Jerusalem, driven from Rhodes by the Turks, took refuge in Malta. And in 1565, Malta's name and Malta's fame first became a symbol of courage. The Grand Master of the Knights, La Valette, with six hundred of his companions and five thousand natives, successfully held Malta against the Turks until aid came from Sicily.

This island has suffered the most intensive bombing of the war, approximately seventeen hundred attacks up to the present. On two occasions it was in the direst peril. To think that when the war broke out there were only three fighter planes on Malta which the inhabitants named Faith, Hope, and Charity! To think that day after day, from out the sun, came hostile planes to attack; and that the closest friends of the island were more than one thousand miles away either in Gibraltar or in Egypt! To think of all this and to consider that Malta still remains unbeaten and untaken is to realize that Malta has given us one of the great stories of the war. Fortunately, all her houses are of stone construction and, even though destroyed, they did not burn. Three out of every four houses in Valletta have been damaged, and the other two cities of Vittoriosa and Senglea are ruins.

Because of the character of the construction and the strong shelters, the casualties were comparatively few. Only fifteen hundred people have been killed in Malta which though deplorable, is surprising because Malta with the exception of Monaco is the most densely populated of any country, with two thousand, two hundred twenty persons to the square mile. New York State has about two hundred and sixty persons to the square mile!

I was happy to have this opportunity to visit Malta, for I had never been there before. Lord Gort is the Governor General, and both His Excellency and his staff made me feel completely at home. He seems to me to be the embodiment of Malta's unconquerable spirit. He is above the age of commanders of armies in combat service, but any one of the younger generals would find himself pressed to equal in activity this man who has not only the military responsibility for Malta's defense, but also for the administration of her civic affairs. Lord Gort is a reserved, but nevertheless a friendly man. He plans everything with the greatest detail. As soon as I reached Malta, he handed me a two-page schedule of a suggested program for my two-day stay, and asked me if I approved of it. Of course I did. And on most of my trip he accompanied me and did his own work in snatches while so generously giving his time to me.

The 15th of April was George Cross Day in Malta, the day on which the civilian Victoria cross was conferred by the King, not on an individual or individuals but on the whole people, "to bear witness to a heroism and devotion that will long be famous in history." I said Mass that morning in the Cathedral, the church of the Knights of Malta. In this Mass, naturally, I prayed for the members of the American association of the Knights of Malta, both living and dead, every single one of whom I know or knew personally.

After breakfast at the Governor's he accompanied me, or rather started to accompany me, in an auto on a four-mile drive. Everywhere along the way children were assembled, and I decided to walk the greater part of the distance. I received bouquets of flowers, enough to cover the floor of the auto. Also, I received spiritual bouquets. One child gave me a small American flag that her teacher, an American Sister stationed in Malta, had brought from our homeland. I was happy to have it; I shall keep it always.

I visited the dockyard. Admiral Mackenzie, in charge of the area, accompanied me on an hour's tour of the docks and shops. When I spoke a few brief sentences to the assembled workers, they all greeted me most warmly. Because of frequent air raids, these workers and their families live in tunnels that they have themselves hewn or that were hewn in past forgotten ages. There were chambers cut in the tunnels, and families live in them; in every niche there is a little shrine, generally of Our Lady of Victory. For three years they have endured this manner of living. While I was visiting the dockyard, there was a drill with gas masks. Every one donned them and kept working. Malta is taking no chances. She has every possible bit of her lands under cultivation, for she knows the value of food; every one from Lord Gort and Archbishop Caruana is strictly rationed for everything.

Lord Gort went with me to Senglea, which is a city of the dead, just as dead as if it had been destroyed a thousand years ago. There were no traces that anything had happened recently, no traces of household objects or personal belongings or charred wood or any of the usual evidences that one sees in bombed areas; just huge blocks of stone that might have been there for ages, such as one would find in Rome, Athens, or other places in the ancient world.

The parish priest took Lord Gort and me to the ruins of his historic Church of Our Lady of Victories, which the Knights of Malta built to commemorate the defeat of the Turks. The priest has burrowed into the ruins and has made a little chapel for some few hundred dwellers in the caves.

It was most impressive to hear the story of the defense of Malta from those who had participated in it, to hear from them about the raids averaging four each day for well-nigh two years, to hear of the turn in the tide, when finally fighter planes arrived in Malta from English and American carriers, and offered the first opposition to the surprised attacking forces, which lost three out of four of its planes. The Battle of Malta was won then and there, and for long periods since there have been only "nuisance raids," as they are called. Malta is now on the offensive, and the Germans and Italians in Tunisia must surrender, for Tunisia will not be a Dunkirk.

Archbishop Caruana brought me to several churches and religious institutions and also to see the bay where St. Paul was shipwrecked. Never in any place in the world, with the exception of Ireland, have I seen such large numbers of evidently devout people as in Malta.

Lord Gort arranged for me to meet all the members of his military and civilian staff either at luncheon or dinner, and also at the ceremony in honor of George Cross Day in the Palace Square at Valletta. This ceremony resembled a medieval pageant. Lord Gort, Archbishop Caruana, other guests, and myself were on the balcony over the main entrance to the Palace. Down in the Square were military bands and representations from the various army and navy units, including Malta's own regiment. Framing the bands and the soldiers and sailors, were the spectators and, beyond, the framework of the bomb-scarred buildings of the Square.

Among those whom I met was the Lieutenant Governor, Mr. D. C. Campbell. He is Lord Gort's civilian aide. Because of Malta's status as an island fortress in the middle of the Mediterranean, the Governor General's military aide is always a naval officer. This position is held at present by Captain Clarke.

Lieutenant Governor Campbell had just arrived in Malta from Uganda. He gave me much information that was very interesting, for I expect to visit all of Africa. In the beginning, I intended to go to India and China immediately after my trip to the Middle East but, as I told you, since I received an invitation from General Smuts to come to South Africa, on my way there I am going through the whole continent as thoroughly as possible, for I know that I shall never have another opportunity to do so.

In Malta, and in every other place recently visited, I have seen how disastrous the war is for Italy. Malta's people are hostile to Mussolini's people, and it is pathetic to think of the damage the Fascist chief has done to civilization and to his own country. If he had only hearkened to the Holy Father, President Roosevelt, and Mr. Churchill, if he had only known the power of England and the United States, if he had only done what was the right thing to do, he would not have treacherously and tragically betrayed and ruined his country, and gravely injured us.

How bitingly prophetic was Winston Churchill in his message to the Italian people, December 23, 1940. It is now placarded on buildings in Tripoli and Malta. It is so striking that I copied these two paragraphs:

It is all because of one man—one man and one man alone has ranged the Italian people in deadly struggle against the British Empire and has deprived Italy of the sympathy and intimacy of the United States of America. . . .

It is all one man—one man, who, against the crown and royal family of Italy, against the Pope and all the authority of the Vatican and of the Roman Catholic Church, against the wishes of the Italian people who had no lust for this war; one man has arrayed the trustees and inheritors of ancient Rome upon the side of the ferocious pagan barbarians. . . .

On the evening of April 15th, my last evening in Malta, Lord Gort gave a farewell dinner for me to which he invited his military and civic aides.

I was up at four o'clock the next morning and celebrated Mass at five o'clock in the parish church of Attard, where the Governor's residence, St. Antoine Palace, is situated. The church was thronged to its capacity, and I was reminded of Mission Masses years ago in Whitman when we would all get up in time to walk to church for five o'clock Mass and instruction, and then walk back home again for breakfast, so that you and everybody else in town could be working at seven o'clock.

In taking leave of Malta, I knew that the Knights of Malta in America, of which I am the Chaplain, would wish me to do something charitable in their name and with their means, so I gave Lord Gort and Archbishop Caruana a check for five thousand dollars to provide extra rations of milk for the children of the island.

Once more I was back in the transparent nose of the airplane looking down and reflecting on the epic of Malta, a symbol of knighthood, charity, and courage. Soon the rim of Africa appeared. We passed over Homs, with the ships sunk in its harbor, trenches bitten into its sands, and gardens sweated into the desert by Italian peasants. Along the shores of the Mediterranean, we flew back to one of its jewels which is Tripoli. I made quick connections for Medenine, going in a battle-scarred Liberator plane just returning to the front after repairs.

General Strickland was going up forward, too, and he piloted his own fighter plane and went along with the Liberator. The front had already passed beyond Medenine, where the engagement had been disastrous for Rommel and the occasion of his abandonment of the Mareth line.

That afternoon I said Mass for the ——— Fighter Group camped not far from El Djem, near Kairouan. The famous Roman Coliseum, built nearly two thousand years ago, was visible. I can write all this because I shall not send any letters to you until all the news is old. But news becomes old very fast, especially in this area where the Allies are making rapid and steady progress, and the end of the battle of Tunis is not more than four or five weeks away.

The Liberator in which I was flying belonged to the 12th Bomber Group. The Chaplain of that outfit, Father McGarity, returned with me that night to Sfax where we occupied one of the few rooms in the town that were left intact. Of course, there was no electric light in Sfax but Father McGarity and I had some candles. We had also some tea, sugar, and a can of Spam, so we had a good meal. We ate the Spam as it came out of the can, without broiling, boiling, frying, hashing, or souffle-ing it. The room was another one of those in which Rommel had slept, but this time he or some one else had taken along the bed, so we both used sleeping rolls, which were fine, but whether they were fine or not, we were lucky to have them.

The next morning we said Mass in a temporary refuge for a Community of Sisters who had been bombed from their convent with the loss of only one life. We visited the harbor area, and then flew on to the most advanced airfield in operation. From there we went forward in an auto over roads but lately used by retreating German troops. All bridges had been blown up. Scorpion mine detectors were operating to make places ready for troop encampments. These are tractors with an apparatus that whips the ground in all directions to detonate the mines. The British have perfected a very fine electrical apparatus that works like a carpet sweeper. The men operating it, wearing earphones, are warned when anything metallic is buried in the ground. When a mine is located, experienced sappers remove it. Now the Germans are using bakelite containers for the mines instead of metallic ones, thus rendering this apparatus useless. It is amazing to see the tremendous number of mines that have

been used to slow up the Allied advance. They are very dangerous to handle, and only this week the British officer most experienced in mine-detecting was killed.

At the Advanced Headquarters of the Desert Air Task Force,
I was the guest of Colonel Thomas Darcy, who lived in All
Saints Parish, Roxbury, when I was stationed there. We were
encamped not far from Sousse, which is a completely devastated
city. It is also a deserted city, as the Germans had just recently
abandoned it and the Allies were moving up. It is on the site
of the ancient city of Susa which was founded before Carthage.
Hannibal took refuge here after his defeat by Scipio in the Battle of Zama, one of the world's decisive battles fought in this
same section.

I am not collecting any souvenirs on this trip, but I did pick
up a German paper published in Munich only two weeks ago
for the German troops in Tunisia, and every one to whom I
have shown it has found it interesting.

Tom Darcy drove me to Sousse on Palm Sunday and was one
of those in attendance at the service. The Liberator plane in
which I flew to the airfield nearest the front was called "Old
War Horse," and the bombing force to which it belonged is
called "Earthquakers." One readily admits the aptitude of the
name when one sees the damage wrought in Sfax and Sousse,
with boats sunk and overturned, buildings crumbled, trains
overturned and destroyed, and with streets a mass of rubbish
and rubble.

I have seen many ghastly sights. In harbors filled with broken
ships, some of them still smoking, some over on their sides
like the *Normandie*, others with masts just protruding, some
with prow up, and some stern up: all bizarre monuments to

man's great ingenuity in construction and destruction. It was a weird sight to see dead camels and other animals, partially skeletonized by burning, along the roadside with crippled tanks, worthless cannon, wrecked camions, and lorries.

The camouflage for the airplanes in the Western Desert Air Forces is pink instead of the green with which we are familiar in the States, as pink blends softly into the desert colors. These planes are called "pink elephants."

During these days I was able to visit the three combat units of the Ninth Air Force, and for the 79th Fighter Group I offered Mass for its first Commander, Colonel Peter McGoldrick, and others of the unit who had been lost.

Evidences of the war and war's ruin are everywhere, even in the desert, for war has passed through this area so recently that the sands have not yet covered its wounds, its scars, and its debris. The honored dead are laid to rest, sometimes gathered together in little cemeteries, sometimes buried, as in the case of airplane accidents, upon the site where the plane crash occurred. These crashes occasion most trying tasks for the Chaplains. Just today I learned of one performed by Father Francis J. Early, of the diocese of Indianapolis. A plane that had crashed was undiscovered for over six weeks. It was finally located high on the side of a precipitous mountain. Father Early and soldiers with him climbed the mountain, with loose shale and narrow shelves for footing, and finally reached the bodies of the victims. They were identified and buried, and crosses were placed over their graves. One soldier told me that going up was not so difficult, and that the entire party slept on the plateau the night following the burial services. But the effect of looking down as they descended was so unsteadying that they all agreed they could have done this precise task only once without catastrophe to themselves.

As the Germans and the Italians retreated into Tunisia they abandoned great quantities of materials. This fact and other indications reveal that the Germans are in a desperate condition and cannot resist much longer. All the Allied Commanders give credit to Rommel, and more credit to him for his retreat than for his advances. It is the opinion of some of the highest officers that, if Rommel had contented himself with advancing to Benghazi or Tobruk, Malta definitely could not have resisted, and Rommel's own lines of communication and supply would have been extremely secure. One of the things showing that all is not well with the German and Italian war machines—at least, not as well as it was formerly—is the fact that among the abandoned supplies are bombs made of concrete. These crude bombs with metal fins bolted to them are uneconomic in a military sense because they do not cause damage proportionate to the danger incurred. In the earlier days of Nazi war domination all bombs were of machine-tooled steel.

By jeeps, peeps, autos, and planes, I returned to Tripoli for one night. I met Major General Lewis H. Brereton that night. He has been stationed all over the world and at present commands in the Middle East. He is a general who goes about everywhere to see conditions for himself. He is small, stocky, alert, incisive, and seems full of compressed energy. In honor of General Brereton's visit, General Strickland had a special dinner with flower decorations on the table in the form of a propeller; we also had ice cream, which was the first I had since leaving the States.

Once more I am in the air on my way from Tripoli to

Benghazi, following the Mediterranean coastline, seeing occasional convoys of ships in the water and trucks on the roads; seeing the sand dunes of the desert in ripples, in waves, and in mountains; seeing occasional groups of nomads that have escaped destruction in the onrushings of armies; seeing great stretches of sand, great patches of salt, occasional splashes of vegetation.

We went along the line of march of Rommel and Montgomery. The plane flew very low, and it was easy to recall different stages and different stories of the long advances and long retreats. The pilot circled over the Marble Arch, which Mussolini had erected to show the dividing line between Tripolitania and Cyrenaica. There will be no more retreats, for the combination of the British Eighth Army and the American Ninth Air Force is definitely and decisively irresistible.

Colonel Euzal G. Ent, Commander of the 98th Bomb Group, and Father Broussard, of Alexandria, Louisiana, the Chaplain of this outfit stationed at Benghazi, met me in the airport and drove me to camp. Colonel Ent gave me the good news that General Crawford and Colonel Cheeves, whom I knew in America, had arrived in North Africa. I was glad to see them and General Crawford became my roommate in another one of Rommel's rooms.

In Benghazi, it was interesting to see the English chalk marks over the German chalk marks, indicating quarters of various officers. The Americans would not bother to rub out the old marks, but simply wrote over them the corresponding American command.

Colonel Ent and Father Broussard brought me to the dock area of Benghazi and we visited the Cathedral, and also the Italian hospital, where I talked with the priests and Sisters.

The American and English bombardment of Benghazi had been terrific, and the Germans also had contributed their quota; but the worst damage to the harbor was wrought by the bombardment of a tidal wave and hurricane which breached the Italian sea wall and tossed many ships to destruction.

I offered Mass in the morning in one of the parish churches in Benghazi. It was filled to capacity with soldiers. I spoke briefly, and met all of them. After Mass, Colonel Ent arranged for me to visit Barce and Tocra, where I called on the interned Bishops of Benghazi and Derna. The Bishop of Benghazi was ill in the hospital with heart trouble and did not feel able to return to his diocese. He was glad to see me but I was sad to see him. The mountain passes along the coastal country through which we drove are high and dangerous, and the retreating army had destroyed many of the bridges. The territory had been bitterly defended, and in the Tocra Pass one whole brigade had been annihilated. Wrecked planes, abandoned trucks and materials are everywhere. My companion that day was Father Smith, an English Chaplain who had been with the Eighth Army since before the zero hour at nine o'clock, October 23rd, when the bombardment prelude to the battle of El Alamein began.

Making our trip with detours around blown-up bridges, through arid wastes, through groves and fields spotted with yellow and red poppies, through herds of cattle, sheep, and goats, through cactus growths and past huts and walls with fading wisteria and flaming bougainvillea, we returned to Benghazi where Colonel Ent was waiting to take me to the airport. There was a B-25, a four-motored Liberator plane, leaving Benghazi for Cairo on a routine flight, and I was a passenger on it.

It was a most interesting experience, for the pilot of the plane,

Colonel Chris H. W. Reuter, of Florida, was extremely familiar with the territory and its history. He was considerate and informative. We circled over the city, over the "River Styx," and over Derna again. We flew at low altitude, and saw everything with almost as great detail as if we were in an automobile. We circled several times over the harbor and city of Tobruk, over El Alamein, and all the places that we read about during the North African campaign. Finally we were over the Nile and Cairo. It had been a fascinating, history-saturated day, a beautiful, cloudless day. It was April's full-moon night, April 20th, and Cairo seemed like a dream city and the Nile like a river of silver.

On my arrival in Cairo, I went to the Apostolic Delegation where I was received by Reverend Arthur Hughes, the Chargé d'Affaires. Other members of the staff were Reverend Francis Anderson, a Jesuit from Boston; and Monsignor Charles Perico, of Vatican City. It was a congenial household and they made me one with themselves.

Father Hughes was born in London; in early manhood he became a convert to the Church. He decided to become a missionary priest, joined the White Fathers in Africa, and studied in their seminary at Algiers where he was ordained. Sent to Uganda, he served there faithfully and successfully for many years. About a year ago he was placed in charge of the Apostolic Delegation. He has never returned to England, and has never seen his mother, nor any of his other relatives, since he left his home for the missions. If I had only known him when I was in England, I would have been happy to call on his mother. Like most missionaries, he wears a beard, so I am not sure of his age, but I think he is about forty-five years old. He is short, stout, intelligent, full of energy and good will. But his good will has been taxed by some sad situations of which many told me. One was the internment of missionary priests in Egypt: Franciscans, Salesians, and members of other religious orders, who had been born in either Germany or Italy years before any one had ever heard of Hitler or Mussolini. They had come to Egypt in their youth and vigor and dedicated themselves to the education of the children of Egypt and to charitable work among them. They came to Egypt to give themselves for the well-being of the people and the country. They looked for no gain in this man's world except the satisfaction that comes to those whose entire lives are devoted to the selfless service of others. Now these missionaries are penned in, watched by armed guards, kept in forced idleness for more than three years, while their parishes, schools and institutions suffer, and the people they served remain unserved and bewildered.

One of the first things I did in Egypt was to visit these priests. It was a sad experience. In my opinion they have been treated not only arbitrarily and unfairly but also with unnecessary harshness. They wondered, and so did I, why those among them who were sick, were not entitled to the same consideration given to other internees who were not priests.

On this same day I signed the King's Book and called on my friend of many years, Alexander Kirk, the United States Minister to Egypt. I then left Cairo for Jerusalem with Chaplains Morrison, of New York, Singleton, of Fresno, and Carey, of Newark, and some other officers and men who were on leave. It was a two-hour flight from Cairo to the Lydda airport, which is near the old city of Jaffa and the modern city of Tel-Aviv. Mr. Pinkerton, the American Consul at Jerusalem, and Monsignor Oddi, in charge of Jerusalem's Apostolic Delegation, met me at the airport.

I looked forward with longing to my four-day stay in the Holy City, the scene of our Lord's Passion, Death and Resurrection. I realized how privileged I was to be in Jerusalem during Holy Week. Epistles, Gospels, and Psalms take on new and deeper meanings when one has visited Biblical places. Meditation on our Lord's life and on His teaching becomes more fruitful after making the composition of place from memories of the scenes themselves.

Palestine is a rather mountainous country, the general topography of which consists of a central spine running north and south, descending abruptly on the east toward the Lake of Tiberias, the River Jordan, and the Dead Sea, and gradually toward the west and the Mediterranean. But perhaps I am going too much into either topography or geography, even though Monsignor Ready thinks that I do better in geography than in other subjects. He told me once that he had advised some one to differ from me on some point other than geography.

On my arrival in Jerusalem, I went with Monsignor Oddi to visit the Patriarch, Archbishop Barlassina. He was pleased to see me, and invited me to officiate at the Holy Sepulchre services on Easter Sunday, and I accepted with gratitude. He invited me also to pontificate on Holy Saturday, at the Holy Sepulchre, and to carry out all the ceremonies of the ritual.

The next day, Holy Thursday, I went to the Cenacle to say Mass. The original Cenacle no longer exists, but either on the site itself or near it are two buildings: a new one, the Franciscan Chapel of the Cenacle, and an ancient one, which is in the hands of the Moslems, and which Christians may visit only twice in the year.

The new Franciscan chapel is in the "Upper Room" of the monastery. Offering Mass there gave me the same feeling I had when I offered my first Mass in Rome; a feeling which, despite a conscious restraint of going slowly through the preliminary parts of the Mass, carries one unconsciously, sweepingly, to the moment of Consecration when human lips pronounce divine words "THIS IS MY BODY." Surely it is an ineffable experience to pronounce these words in the very place where Christ, the Great High Priest, uttered them for the first time!

On Thursday afternoon I participated in the Holy Hour in the Church of the Garden of Gethsemane, a shrine built with offerings made on Good Friday by faithful from all over the world. The rock on which tradition says Christ suffered His agony rises out of the pavement of the church just in front of the sanctuary. The Basilica is built on a ledge foundation, of which this protruding rock is a part. It is easy to meditate during a Holy Hour in this place, on this day, the eve of Good Friday, with the rock of the agony before one's vision, and with the liturgical prayers of the Church stimulating one's mind, heart, and soul.

On Good Friday morning, I visited Gethsemane again and saw the garden, the olive trees, and the grotto, and in mid-morning I led the Stations of the Cross for hundreds of soldiers, going from one station to another along the road of the Passion to the Mount of Calvary. Soldiers from every allied country were in the pilgrimage; and all of us, I know, felt the tug of our homelands, and were strengthened to carry our own crosses.

I need not go into detail in regard to all the places that I visited in Jerusalem. They had always been part and parcel of my life even though I had never seen them before. The first seeds of knowledge in my mind, the first things I learned at home from mother and you, were backgrounded in this Holy Land. Easter Sunday morning was, of course, the culminating joy. The ceremonies were carried out with all the beauty of the liturgy of a Pontifical Mass with a reverence and deep realization of its significance.

The American Consul, Mr. Lowell W. Pinkerton, and Mrs. Pinkerton invited me and all American members of the Franciscan Order residing in Jerusalem to have luncheon with them. After an enjoyable hour together I drove to the Dead Sea and the River Jordan, near the Mount of Christ's temptation. I crossed the Jordan and went into Trans-Jordania toward the mountain from which Moses viewed the Promised Land and I returned to Jerusalem for an evening meal with the Patriarch, to whom I then bade farewell.

I had prepared a broadcast for America. Unfortunately, atmospheric conditions prevented its transmission, but I include it here since it contains reflections that I have had in the Holy Land, and considerations which I believe are helpful in our war for peace:

On Good Friday, I followed from station to station the footsteps of Jesus Christ as He endured the Agony of His Passion and Crucifixion. Through the streets of Jerusalem to the Mount of Calvary I went, and there did I meditate that Christ came on earth to teach man to love God and to live and die at peace with God and neighbor.

I visited the traditional spot where Jesus wept over Jerusalem, as He foresaw the city beaten flat to the ground with not a stone left upon a stone because she did not know the time of her visitation. I thought of Christ weeping over the greater Jerusalem that is all the world today. You and I are participating in the passion and crucifixion of the human race. We are in the Gethsemane of civilization. Never before has there been anything comparable to the present efficiency in destruction of human lives, in upheavals of peoples, in misery, and in devastation whose stains and ruins are inerasable.

Christ had His agony; and so has each one of us and so has our country. From the depths of our sufferings we must rise and our country must rise if civilization is to survive. Of the military victory of the Allied Nations in this war, there is no doubt. I do not imply that I think victory is either proximate or easy. For those who started this war, although they see the handwriting on the wall, in the air, on the land and on the sea, nevertheless are fighting with a desperation impelled by something different from patriotism. They know that the allied terms are "unconditional surrender," but they interpret "unconditional surrender" by definitions from their own dictionaries; and America's dictionary, unless we get a new edition, means justice for all; and *all* includes enemies if we are to be just to ourselves and just to posterity.

It is well for us to bear in mind that victory is not synonymous with peace. This Humpty-Dumpty world has had a very great fall. Hatreds have multiplied and intensified. Yet Easter Day should not and must not pass without hope. Hope must be based on faith, supernatural faith. Faith and hope beget charity, and charity means peace.

Humanly speaking, the foundation of peace is contented peoples. The average man in every country is contented if he can earn his living and support his family with tranquillity. But also, humanly speaking, we know now or we should know that something more than brains, brawn, machines and material is needed to bring peace to mankind. These can give us and these will give us victory. But they cannot give us peace after the victory if we reject the cornerstone of the building of peace, which is Jesus Christ.

I address myself to all those who believe in God; and only the fool says in his heart there is no God. For those who do not acknowledge Jesus as the Son of God must nevertheless recognize in His personality, His doctrines and His commandments, His Sermon on the Mount, a sure and indestructible basis on which world brotherhood under the fatherhood of God may be firmly established.

Here in this Holy Land I pray not only for victory but for peace. All believers in God, all men of good will, can unite in this prayer for peace. They can also contribute to its realization by thinking, working, speaking, writing, teaching, learning, and living in the presence of God, by making Christ the cornerstone of the building of their lives, by making Christ the cornerstone of the building of peace.

Monday morning at five o'clock I celebrated Mass in the Chapel of the Nativity in Bethlehem, and visited the Church and the Monastery. It was dark when we left Jerusalem for Bethlehem, and stars studded the sky. Neither Monsignor Oddi nor I said one word. I was thinking, as I am sure he was also, of that night, on yonder hillside, in that little village, when Christ was born. The Scriptures say, "The world knew Him not." Nor does the world know Him today.

Later, I visited the ruins of the Temple of Solomon, and the Wailing Wall, and then departed for Mount Tabor. Just before I left Jerusalem, I went to the roof of the Delegation, and spent some time looking over the city which I believed I was seeing for the last time. With Mount Sion and the Cenacle in the foreground, I followed in my vision and in my thought the line of the street down which our Lord went to Gethsemane, I looked from the house of Caiaphas to the tower "Antonia," where Christ appeared before Pilate, and thence to the house of Herod and back to Pilate again, where He was condemned to death. I followed Christ to Calvary once more, and with my eyes fixed on the place of crucifixion, I said a final prayer that God in His mercy would stop the swinging of the scythe of war.

Father Pascal, an American Franciscan, President of Terra Sancta College, allowed me the use of his automobile and permitted Brother Anthony Bruya to accompany me to other places in Palestine. From the map I made up an itinerary. Mount Tabor looked easily accessible but the map did not show the condition of the road! An amphibian jeep or a camel would have been better means of transportation than an auto, for there was no road to merit the name, and furthermore there were a few streams to ford. But after we had reached the base of Tabor there was a fairly good road to the top of the mountain, and arriving there made us forget all our difficulties. Tabor is a great mountain built by God in the great sanctuary which is the world, and it is wonderful to gaze at the panorama which the eyes of our Blessed Lord Himself beheld. One sees the plain of Esdraelon and one thinks of our present Armageddon. Scripture was written among the hills and dales of all this countryside and today I could read it here. For one says instinctively with the Apostles before whom Christ was transfigured on Tabor: "Lord, it is good for us to be here."

The Franciscans in the monastery on the top of Tabor served luncheon for us. One of them is Brother Julian, of Westerly, Rhode Island. To him I was a breath from home, and he was a breath of sanctity to me. Together we went to the basilica church on the mountain top. It is an unusual marble and alabaster church built only a few decades ago.

From Tabor we went down the hill to Tiberias on the Sea of Galilee, where once more we stayed with the Franciscan Fathers. I received the warmest possible welcome, not only from them, but also from the Polish children who are refugees living in their school convent. It was late afternoon but I was anxious to take a ride on the lake. The Father Superior hired a little motorboat, and we went from Tiberias nearly to Capernaum. I wanted to do nothing but think about the different scenes of the Gospel that took place on this lake. Jesus had walked along these shores. In the midst of a storm on these waters, He had said to His Apostles: "Be of good heart. It is I. Fear not." We could see the

Mount of the Beatitudes where He gave the only model for any charter of human rights and duties that will ever work!

I wished to be at Nazareth on the following morning, but, because the Polish children wanted me to be with them, I attended Mass in the parish church and distributed Holy Communion to them. In Nazareth, in the Grotto of the Church of the Annunciation, on the altar on which was carved, "Here the Word was made flesh," I offered Mass.

It is wonderful to say the Hail Mary in the Church of the Annunciation in Nazareth. It is wonderful to say the Franciscan Rosary in the place where the Hail Mary means the most, at the Tomb of the Virgin near the Garden of Gethsemane; wonderful to say seventy-two Hail Marys in honor of our Blessed Mother, representing her traditional age. It is like a foretaste of heaven to offer Mass in the Grotto of the Nativity, where it is written, "Here, of the Virgin Mary, Jesus Christ was born."

After leaving the Church of the Annunciation in Nazareth, I went to the college of the Salesian Fathers where many Polish boys are quartered. They are orphans aged from twelve to eighteen and they are being taught the usual high school subjects by Polish teachers. I spent an hour with them, and then returned to Galilee, stopping at Cana, where our Lord wrought His first miracle.

There was a long journey before us, as we were on our way to Damascus, so, shortly after luncheon, we left by automobile, stopping at the Chapel of St. Peter. On this very spot Christ made Peter the head and the cornerstone of His Church where we all said a prayer for Peter's successor, our Holy Father. We had a frontier to cross from Palestine into Syria before we reached Damascus, the capital of Syria, believed to be the oldest city of the world that is still inhabited.

In every town we entered on the way to Damascus, French troops were drawn up in salute, and the automobile was escorted by cavalry. In Damascus, there was a squad of soldiers on camels, and the entire street near St. Joseph's Church, where I was to stop, was lined with soldiers at attention. I appreciated this consideration, but I was disturbed by it because I did not know how long they had been waiting. Since I did not know myself when I was going to arrive, I didn't see how any one else could know, but I found out that word had been sent from the frontier.

The Commander of the area is General Collet. Shortly after my arrival we exchanged calls, and the next day the General and his wife entertained us at luncheon. The old pastor of the Church, Father Joseph, is a Belgian. The only other two priests left in the monastery after the ravages of the war are Dutch and Yugoslav. Father Joseph looked like a picture of St. Joseph.

Wednesday morning I spent in visiting places of interest in Damascus. It was somewhat of a task to persuade the guide to bring me to the places I wanted to see instead of to the places he wished me to see. But finally, despite my traditional meekness, I succeeded in going where I wanted to go and seeing what I wanted to see, including the spot where the conversion of St. Paul took place, and the principal mosque in Damascus. Immediately after luncheon we left Damascus for Beirut.

I wished to stop in Baalbek. Contemplating the vastness of the ruins of the Temple of Baal, and seeing the evidences of its former grandeur and magnificence fill one with awe. This Temple of Baal, in the old city of Heliopolis, is said to have taken over three hundred years to build. One of the stones is supposed to be the largest quarried stone in the world, weighing approximately eleven hundred tons. Any surface of it is larger than New York's largest slab in the west sidewalk of Fifth Avenue, near Fifty-first Street.

After Baalbek, we resumed our journey to Lebanon, the only Levant State that I had not yet visited. The same range of mountains that forms the backbone of Palestine, runs north and south along the borders of Syria and Lebanon, broadens out and divides into two ranges. Snow-capped Mount Hermon dominates the whole region. It was, in fact, the center of the circle of my travels from the Lake of Tiberias to Damascus, to Beirut, and back to Palestine. The mountain passes are sometimes snow-blocked; and a few weeks earlier it would have been impossible for me to have taken this trip. We passed Rayak, where a great number of our soldiers were formerly encamped, and saw the railway and the tunnels recently constructed by New Zealanders in record time, completing the vital railroad between Cairo and Baghdad.

On the outskirts of Beirut we were met by the Vicar General of the Armenian diocese, Monsignor Kedidjian, who, like the Patriarch, was a student with me in Rome. I was surprised that they both remembered so many of their American associates.

The Patriarch himself, Gregory Peter XV, was a classmate, whose name in those days was Francis Agagianian. Despite his sorrows, his worries, and cares, he looks much younger than I do. I noticed that the cross he wore is similar to one that Pius XI gave me when I was consecrated a Bishop. The Patriarch told me that Pius XI had given him his cross, also.

We talked of our former professors, our mutual friends, and ourselves. The Patriarch was very glad to see me, for we had been friendly during all the years of our seminary life, and we saw each other occasionally when he lived in Rome as the rector of the Armenian College. He also held the chair of Sacramental Theology at the Roman University where we were students together.

Millions of Armenians have been slain or sent into exile during the past few decades, but the world does not seem to be aware of the martyrdom of this people. In the courtyard before the Patriarch's residence there is a monument to the memory of the thousands who were massacred in 1939.

The Patriarch felt that I should remain another day because there were so many people whom he wished me to visit, and so many things we wished to discuss. However, I assured him I could do all he wished me to do and still leave the next day as I had planned.

I had called on Mr. Wadsworth, the American Consul, immediately on my arrival, April 28th. He was the American diplomatic official who received notice from Count Ciano that Italy had declared war on the United States. Mr. Wadsworth said that he told Ciano that he was "awfully sorry" and we agreed that Ciano must be "sorrier" today.

The next morning, I went up Mount Lebanon to the seminary and the shrine of the Madonna, and later was received by the President of Lebanon, Alfred Nakkache, Cardinal Tappouni, the French Ambassador, and the Apostolic Delegate. The President had a guard of honor to receive me. He is a simple, unpretentious person. His office is so small and very plainly furnished that he would be a formidable candidate in any worldwide competition of heads of states with smallest offices. President Nakkache has been in America and greatly admires our country. Cardinal Tappouni, the only Cardinal in the Orient, is a Syrian and has lived many years in Rome. In addition to Armenians and Syrians in Lebanon, there are also Maronites and Greeks.

Nearly every one I meet in these small countries seems to be familiar with the Atlantic Charter, more familiar with it, perhaps, than many of us Americans. People in this part of the world see so few Americans these days, that those of us who do come here are questioned closely about it. While there will be great obstacles in putting all its provisions into effect, I have found that men and women everywhere over here believe in it and put their deepest trust in it.

Leaving Lebanon to return to Palestine, we drove south along the Mediterranean, stopping briefly at Sidon and at Tyre. We crossed the frontier into Palestine, passing Acre, reminiscent of the Crusaders and of Napoleon; going through Haifa, a thriving port of Palestine, and finally arriving at Mount Carmel just after sunset. I had supper with the Carmelite Fathers, and in the morning I prayed before the beautiful shrine of Our Lady. The President of the College, Father Edmond O'Callahan, is Irish, very capable, forceful, and well informed.

Saturday, May 1st, we had an early morning start from Mount Carmel and coasted along the Mediterranean shore to the city of Tel-Aviv, the Atlantic City of Palestine. Ten years ago it was just a desert outside the old city of Jaffa. Now it is an ultramodern city inhabited permanently by refugees from Europe, and temporarily by convalescent American soldiers and by airmen on leave from their dangerous nerve-fraying activities. There I met many of our men, and afterwards drove to the British cemetery where some of our American boys are buried.

From Lydda we took a plane for Cairo. We flew over the Suez Canal, circled above and around the pyramids, saw the Sphinx very clearly, and came down to the airport to remain in Cairo a few days before starting on another longer circuit from this cross-roads city.

Sunday morning I had services for over one thousand soldiers at the —— General Hospital and Depot at Heliopolis. After talking with them I went to see the seriously sick in the hospital and I shall make the entire rounds from bed to bed as soon as I am able.

Today is my fifty-fourth birthday. Father Hughes gave a tea at the Delegation and I had an opportunity of meeting many of my countrymen, members of the armed forces as well as British and Polish military and civilian officials.

After every one had gone, I opened a package which Mr. Kirk had left with me and I was surprised and happy to find twenty letters that had been following me. It was the best birthday present I could have received, for it is my first mail from home since I left you all three months ago.

On board the Taurus Express, leaving Turkey
May 19, 1943

My days since my birthday have been as busy as usual. Through the kindness of General Brereton and General Crawford, our American Commanders in the Middle East, I visited all our installations in Egypt, spending several days in the Suez Canal area and returned to Cairo.

Sunday, May 9th, was Mother's Day, and there were many demands upon me. During the day I made four different addresses and met hundreds of soldiers, some of whom I knew in the States. It was also convent-visiting day, and I went to the institutions conducted by the Sisters of the Good Shepherd and the Franciscan Sisters of the Immaculate Conception. The Franciscan Sisters have placed part of their school at the disposition of the soldiers. They invite them to "home dinners" which are certainly appreciated. The boys come not only from the States but from New Zealand, Australia, Canada, from all over the world. These meetings give them opportunities to become acquainted with and accustomed to one another. There are six hundred children in the school. Mother Hilarion Madden from Pittsburgh, the Superior, is a stamp expert and we had a little talk on that inexhaustible subject.

On Sunday evening, I had supper with General Patrick J. Hurley, President Roosevelt's personal representative in North Africa and the Middle East. He is from Oklahoma and was Secretary of war in President Hoover's Cabinet. Tall and soldierly in appearance, he is an extraordinarily interesting talker whether his audience be one person or many.

The next noon I left for Aleppo in Syria. The flight was over territory that had become very familiar to me: Egypt, the Suez Canal region, and the Sinai Peninsula, which is that arrow-shaped land on the eastern side of the Suez Canal jutting down into the Red Sea. The plane followed the coast rather closely until we reached a point in Palestine about halfway between Jaffa and Haifa, and then we turned inland. We passed over Nazareth and close by Mount Tabor, and then followed along the border line between Trans-Jordania and Palestine, meeting the Sea of Galilee just where the River Jordan begins. Once more Mount Hermon and both ranges of the Lebanon Mountains came into view as we crossed over the valley from Syria to Aleppo. We flew low and very close to the ruins of Baalbek, but, even so, they looked diminutive from the air.

In Aleppo I met Lieutenant Tonkin, an Australian attached to the Royal Air Force, and Father Pauvot, the Superior of the Jesuits. They brought me to the convent of the Franciscan Missionaries of Mary. I did not have good news for them as I had heard only that morning that their convent in Algiers, near the Church of Our Lady of Africa, had been bombed and that seventeen of the Sisters, including the Superior, had been killed. They were sad at the news but consoled to learn that the Sisters had been able, before the bombing, to place all the children under their care in a bomb shelter and that not one child had been injured. I have seen the work of the Franciscan Missionaries of Mary in many parts of the world, and I have always had the greatest admiration for them; they truly compose an organi-

zation of efficient, self-sacrificing, saintly women. Since so many
of their institutions are in missionary countries, these Sisters
have been among the great victims of the war.

In this Community in Aleppo, as well as in all other Communities, there are Sisters of many nationalities. They all live
in concord and harmony, unified in religion and in service to
God and man. By its enemies religion has been called a drug.
It is a drug, and furthermore, it is the *only* drug that will counter-
act the virus of hatred now flowing in the blood streams of men
and nations. And these men and women of religion whom I am
meeting every day, labor in the midst of most discouraging circumstances, labor in fields that are parched and flinty, for a
harvest of souls.

At the present time, neither civilian nor military planes are
available for Turkey so I took the Taurus Express from Aleppo
to Istanbul, or rather to Scutari which is on the Asiatic side
of the Bosphorus. The train takes its name from the Taurus
Mountains in Turkey, through which it passes. Aleppo is the
station where the section of the train leaving Baghdad, in Iraq,
is joined to the section that leaves Beirut.

The Express was five hours late leaving Aleppo but at last
we were on our way. Once more my formidable medical certificate stood me in good stead, for as soon as we had crossed
the frontier from Syria into Turkey, a man with a long pin in
his hand went from passenger to passenger, scarifying the skin
of all those who could not produce a recent official vaccination
certificate; then a small boy assistant rubbed a drop of vaccine
into the abrasion.

This was the first *wagon-lit* train that I had been on for a good
many years, and it recalled to mind my favorite European train,

the Rome-Paris Express that I took around the middle of so many Decembers to enable me to reach Whitman for Christmas. In fact, this train was made up of the same cars that were formerly in operation from Rome to Paris.

The train ride afforded me the first opportunity of my trip to have time to read. For, short as the distance looks on the map and quick though the trip would be by air, it is a minimum of two days' train travel in each direction between Aleppo and Scutari. I read a book, some pamphlets that I have gathered, and some American magazines and newspapers. I marvel that the newsmen over here keep the American public so accurately and thoroughly informed.

The Express was due in Scutari Thursday night, May 13th, but it never arrives Thursday night. It generally reaches Scutari some time on Friday morning; but we did not get there until Friday afternoon, about fourteen hours late.

Turkey is in a very difficult position politically. Like every other country, she is concerned about her own interests. The whole Middle East presents very complicated problems. Every country is afraid of some other country. Turkey worries about both Germany and Russia; her policy over the years is to have Turkey for the Turks. It was to carry out this policy some few years ago that the great mass exchange of peoples took place between Turkey and Greece.

We reached Ankara, the present capital of Turkey, late Thursday night. To my surprise, Mr. Laurence Steinhardt, the American Ambassador to Turkey, and Mr. Kelley, the Counsellor of the Embassy, were at the station to meet me. We had a very pleasant visit for the half hour that the train remained in the station; and with pleasure and gratitude I accepted Mr. Steinhardt's invitation to visit him and his wife in Ankara on my return from Istanbul.

From Ankara we continued on to Scutari. My abundant supply of reading matter was the occasion of my meeting many people on the train, for I conducted a miniature magazine exchange. It is possible to see a great deal of Turkey from the car windows because many towns are located on the railway route. We passed through barren wastes and fertile places, over several mountain ranges, and along river beds. At the different stations there were leisurely stops, and soldiers and civilians gathered to meet the train. The Turkish soldier has the reputation of being a brave and hardened soldier, and his appearance confirms his reputation.

The territory of modern Turkey is, of course, replete with memorable events, both religious and historical. On our way we passed through Adana, the place of the recent meeting between Winston Churchill and President Inönü of Turkey. Crossing the River Sehan we were not far from Tarsus, the birthplace of St. Paul. We passed near the site of Cæsar's famous victory over Pharnaces, where he uttered the famous expression: "I came, I saw, I conquered." We had a view of Gordium where Alexander the Great cut the Gordian Knot. Nearby are Nicaea and Chalcedon where the ancient councils of the Church were held, and where now there are hardly any Christians.

Now and then I would stop reading, gaze out of the window, and think back. I did some thinking ahead, too, and the expression about Humpty Dumpty that had occurred to me in Palestine came to my mind again. Humpty Dumpty is not only broken and spattered but he is charred by human greeds and hates. Injustice, poverty, disease, and squalor are increasing and

spreading. Cruelty is becoming normal, and sadism is as viru-
lent and as contagious to the mind as typhus is to the body.
Certainly, we must have a great faith in Faith, for only through
that faith can we penetrate the mystery of life and death.

Formerly, statesmen tried for balances of power to keep peace
among nations; now some statesmen have swung to the theory
that monopolies of power may be solutions to world peace.
But, whatever the theory, it would certainly be a mighty advance
if human beings could regard other human beings, not as pawns
in a game, but as individuals with sacred rights to life and liberty. It sounds like Utopia, and yet there would be enough of
everything for everyone if mankind could find a way in which
to channel its efforts to construction instead of destruction.
Years ago, when I traveled in the Balkans, I saw with my own
eyes and heard with my own ears about various factors that
have made these countries a battleground for centuries. I think
that the problems besetting the Balkans are not so difficult to
adjust as are the clashes of interests in the Middle East.

We shall soon arrive in Scutari, which as I said, is in Asia
across the Bosphorus from Istanbul in Europe. In less than one
week I have been on three continents: Africa, Asia, and Europe.
The Apostolic Delegate, Monsignor Roncalli, was at the station
to meet me, together with the American Consul, Mr. Berry.
I was pleased to see also Monsignor Clarizio, whom I had met
in Lisbon and who had traveled with me to Rome. I had known
Monsignor Roncalli for many years, and it was good to see him
again. We crossed on the ferry from Scutari to Istanbul, and
then went to the Delegation where I left my bag.

Afterwards we drove along the Bosphorus to the entrance of
the Black Sea, and saw on the opposite bank the hospital where

Florence Nightingale nursed the wounded in the Crimean War. We saw the palace that was built especially to receive the chandelier given to the Sultan by Queen Victoria because no existing palace was large enough to receive it. We made visits to the great Church of St. Sophia, which the Turks changed from a Christian place of worship into a mosque, and which Attaturk, one morning, changed from a mosque into a museum.

During my stay in Istanbul I visited Mount Sinai Convent and also several churches. It is forbidden by Turkish law for any church to have an entrance directly on the street. Priests and nuns, with the exception of the Apostolic Delegate, are not permitted to wear religious garb outside of rectories, churches, and convents. As an American visitor I continued to wear mine.

On Sunday, May 16th, I preached brief sermons in English and Italian, in the Cathedral which was filled to capacity and beyond it. At noon, all the prelates of Istanbul were present at luncheon where I met two Armenians who had been in the University with me in Rome. That afternoon I left Istanbul on the boat for Scutari to take the train to Ankara.

Mr. Steinhardt telegraphed a welcome from Mrs. Steinhardt and himself, telling me that they had arranged for me to meet some of their friends and that the President of Turkey was to receive me. The Ambassador and Mr. Kelley met me at the station and brought me to the chapel in the French Consulate, for there are no churches in Ankara. I had a quiet two hours with Ambassador and Mrs. Steinhardt in their beautiful villa before the luncheon guests arrived. I was surprised to see that there were twenty-six guests; I was honored to meet the Ambassadors and Ministers representing all the Allied Powers.

After luncheon, President Ismet Inönü received me in his

palace, a salmon-pink modern building on one of Ankara's hills. The Ambassador was with me. One of the President's chief assistants, Mr. Sevki Berker and his secretary, Mr. Sureya Anderman, were with the President, and Mr. Anderman, who was a graduate of Columbia, acted as interpreter.

President Inönü is a military man, and was an important general of the Turkish army in the time of Ataturk. He is deliberate in speech, always thinking a moment before phrasing a question or giving an answer. All his inquiries, I answered with frankness and to the best of my ability. The President was dressed in formal clothes, and so were Mr. Steinhardt and the others. The protocol for reception by the President of Turkey is very strict concerning requirements for formal dress in audience. One of the Embassy staff had asked me what I would do about this, and I replied that both my formal and informal dress for every occasion were the clothes I had on, and that I was sure there would be no difficulty. And there was none.

In the evening, Mr. and Mrs. Steinhardt had the whole Embassy staff and Consulate, as well as the Military Attachés, present for dinner. Afterwards, all were kind enough to come to the station to see me off. I shall now say "good-bye" to Turkey and "good night" to you.

To make a full record of everything that happens would require that I write a letter every other day. Unfortunately, I get time to write only about once a week to tell you where I have been, where I am going, what I am doing and whom I am seeing.

I closed my last letter saying "good-bye" to Turkey. I said "good morning" to Syria in Aleppo on May 19th, where Father Pauvot met me at the station and brought me to the Jesuit chapel. Afterwards we called on the Greek and Armenian Bishops, of whom I have now met a great many. Later we drove about Aleppo and saw the citadel, which looks very impressive from the ground as it did from the air.

We walked a bit about the city and among the people. As always, I observed the children. They are the best index to every country's future. It is sad to see, in so many places, undernourished, sick, and neglected children. Every country's greatest treasure are her children and it is tragic to see the children of today in many blighted lands climbing into boyhood and girlhood, denied not only food for the body, but also the character food of parental care and guidance. Knowledge and love of God must be the supernatural cement, and love of family and neighbor must be the natural cement, which should make the child a strong and healthy unit of community and nation.

Father Pauvot took me into a bank to get some money changed.

Foreign exchange of money is quite an undertaking nowadays.
One must give the monetary system some attention, especially
if one is traveling in as many countries as I am. For example,
the Turkish pound is valued at 55¢; the Egyptian pound at
$4.16; the Palestinian pound at $4.05; the Syrian and the Libyan
pound, each at 44¢. In Iran, the unit is a toman, which is valued
at 32¢; and it takes ten rials to make a toman. In Iraq, the unit
is a dinar, which is worth $4.03. So you can see how easy it is
to buy a dinner in Persia, pay for it in Iraqian money and
know how much it cost.

It was an easy and pleasant three-hour plane ride from Aleppo
to Baghdad. The distance between these two cities is slightly less
than five hundred air miles; and, for the most part, one follows
the course of the Euphrates River. Baghdad is the capital of
Iraq, formerly known as Mesopotamia, which means "between
the rivers," so called because of the great plain between the
Euphrates and Tigris Rivers. You would like to know that
Baghdad means "gift of God," and Iraq means "a cliff." Just
before arriving at Baghdad, we passed over what is thought to
be the Garden of Eden. I saw nothing about it, either from the
air or afterwards on the ground, that would make the spot cor-
respond to its traditional description. Baghdad itself is located
on the Tigris River, and, as we circled over the city we saw both
the Tigris and the Euphrates, for the narrowest strip of land
divides them. South of the city they flow apart again forming
an ellipse and actually meet some three hundred miles farther
to the southeast of Baghdad and flow together into the Persian
Gulf.

At the airport, I inquired the name of the best hotel in
Baghdad, at that moment being in the frame of mind that I

thought the best was none too good. I was told it was the Tigris Palace. The name was certainly pleasant-sounding. On my arrival there, the man at the desk, observing that I was a priest, asked me, "Why don't you stop at Baghdad College?" This seemed surprisingly poor salesmanship, but I took the suggestion and telephoned to the College. Father Sargeant, a Jesuit from Boston, answered the telephone and said that the American Minister, Mr. Wilson, expected me to stay with him, and, in fact, had made preparations for me to do so.

Forthwith I went to the Minister's residence on the outskirts of the city. It was a large, substantial building with a portico built about six years ago. The owner evidently was a competent business man, for he rented it so profitably that he has already reimbursed himself for the price of the land and the building, and the American Government is fortunate to have leased it because other places are unavailable. Naturally, he will not sell it, for the Iranians are well aware that real property, personal property, any property, is more valuable than money.

America is represented in Iraq by Thomas Murray Wilson, an able, experienced and efficient public servant. During the two days I spent in Baghdad, we came to know and like each other. He is a career man in the Diplomatic service and has spent much time in the Middle Eastern countries and at the Middle East desk in the Secretariate of State in Washington and he told me many interesting things about the Arab world. His sister, an Episcopalian nun, Sister Elspeth, C.S.N., is stationed in St. Mary's Convent, Peekskill, New York.

Shortly after my arrival, Father Sargeant came to see me and together we went to call on the Apostolic Delegate, Archbishop de Jonghe, a Belgian priest of the Lazarist Order. He spent many

years as a missionary in China, and of China he speaks with
real affection. In the evening I was Mr. Wilson's guest at a buffet
supper and I met many of his friends and colleagues.

The next morning, I was up very early to fly about fifty miles
from Baghdad to Habbaniya, to celebrate Mass for three thousand Polish soldiers. Bishop Gawlina, the Chaplain General of
the Polish Army, went with me. The soldiers gave me a beautiful
silver chalice which I used at the Mass. I was touched by the
gift, its beauty and its significance.

I flew back to Baghdad, arriving in time to go with Mr. Wilson
to an eleven o'clock audience with the Prince Regent of Iraq.
When we went into the audience, we did not know whether
we were to see the Prince Regent or his brother, so Mr. Wilson
told me that if he said, "Royal Highness," it would be the regent
and if he said, "Highness," it would be his brother. He said
"Royal Highness." Then I knew that it was the Prince Regent,
H.R.H. Abdul Ilah.

We spent half an hour with him. He is a young man with a
pleasing personality, much interested in America and very
anxious to go there for a visit. He is ruling for the young king,
who is only seven or eight years old. We then called on the
Prime Minister, General Nuri-as-Sa'id, and a strong man, physi-
cally as well as politically, who has a wide influence among the
Arabs, even with those outside of Iraq.

The luncheon to which the British Ambassador, Sir Kinahan
Cornwallis, and Lady Cornwallis had invited Mr. Wilson and
me, afforded additional opportunities to learn about the Arab
world from men and women who have lived many years in various places in the Middle East.

Immediately after luncheon, Bishop Gawlina, two Polish

Chaplains and I took the long, hot, dusty ride to Babylon. I knew that the ruins of Babylon are not impressive; I knew that the ride there would be unpleasant; and finally I knew that I was terribly tired. But I knew, also, that even if there were only some old bricks to be seen, I would not fail to go there. This region was the cradle of humanity, the site of the Tower of Babel, of Balthazar's feast, and also of the lions' den into which Daniel the Prophet was cast. How well do I remember you in my very youngest days, teaching me Bible History, and the book you bought me with the engravings of Gustave Doré so that I could more easily remember what you told me. Many of the episodes illustrated in that book took place in Babylon; and to Babylon I went, and was well repaid. German archaeologists have made extensive excavations, and the identification of various places has been convincingly established. Bishop Gawlina had been a Scripture professor and an archaeological student. He and the curator were saturated with facts and theories and they sprinkled a few more on me than I was able to absorb.

That evening, back in Baghdad, we had an outdoor buffet supper at the Apostolic Delegation, to which were invited Mr. Wilson and his staff, the various clergy of Baghdad and some Americans residing in the city. This garden party provided a pleasant, effective way to meet a large number of people.

On the morning of Friday, May 21st, I said Mass at Baghdad College, which is staffed with Jesuits from New England. Needless to say, I enjoyed being with them; and for them and for the way in which they are doing their work, I have great admiration. They have a fine, modern establishment, the gift of an anonymous American. Iraqi boys from Baghdad, and beyond, have thronged to this College, anxious to have the instruction provided by these teachers from the United States. The appreciation of the boys and their parents is a compensation and a consolation to these priests who have left their homeland, many of them, forever. Supplies and replacements are difficult to get. Keeping the College going is a continuing problem. When I was there, the faculty was greatly worried because the auto-busses in which they bring the boys to school are old and worn, like the one-horse shay. If they break down, the school breaks up.

The founder of the College was Father Rice, of Framingham, Massachusetts, now Apostolic Delegate in Honduras. I officiated at his consecration in Boston just a few days before it was announced I was to be Archbishop of New York. One of the priests at Baghdad College, Father Madaras, gave me an enjoyable book containing letters that he had written home, describing the founding and the early years of the college from 1932 to 1936.

I had half a day to drive and walk around the city of Baghdad, to see living conditions and to try to get an idea about economic conditions. One idea I got was that an automobile tire in the black market costs about one thousand dollars in Iraqian money! In recent years, many improvements have been made in Baghdad. Now, for example, there is asphalt on the main street. Up to a few years ago, in order to cross this street in the rainy season, one had to be carried on the back of a Kurd. These Kurds are strong men from the mountains, who, strong though they are and united though they would like to be, are now living divided in Turkey, Iraq, Iran and Afghanistan.

In the afternoon I left Baghdad for Basra on the Persian Gulf, a flight of three hundred miles. On the trip we flew over Babylon, over Ur, the birthplace of Abraham, and circled Basra, the port of Sinbad the Sailor. At the airport, I met the command ing officer, Colonel Johnson, and the American Consul, Mr. Fletcher. A number of priests from the area were there also: Father Torney, an American military chaplain, Father Merrick, an American Jesuit, and Father Conlon, a chaplain of the Royal Air Force.

Basra is a terrifically hot place. With the heat and dust storms, flea bites and other kinds of bites, Basra can keep one uncomfortable. Because of the great heat in this region and the consequent loss of body salts, every one is obliged to take six salt tablets a day. Father Merrick and Father Torney went with me to visit hospitals, encampments, churches and institutions in Basra. Across the combined Euphrates and Tigris Rivers, I went to Khorramshahar and Abadan in Iran; places of which we never heard when we studied geography, but which will be remembered for at least two generations by Americans, who have sweated out portions of their lives in our war effort.

General Hurley was in Basra, and it was pleasant meeting him again. We were guests of Colonel Johnson at dinner and were afterwards invited to speak to the officers.

I was informed that General Connolly, the Commander-in-Chief of the American Forces in the Persian Gulf, was expecting me on Saturday, May 22nd, so I left on that day for Tehran, the capital city of Iran. This was one of the most pleasant stops on my trip. The cordiality of the welcome was preluded by a telegram from General Connolly in which he said: "I take great pleasure in inviting you and your retinue to stay at my official residence as my guests during your stay in Tehran. Subject to your approval, we have made tentative plans to have you celebrate a Field Mass for this Command on Sunday morning at

Camp Amiradab. I look forward to meeting you at the airport."
When General Connolly met me at the airport, he laughed
because I had no "retinue" for him to accommodate. He took
me to his residence and I felt completely at home all the time I
was there. Those living in the house with General Connolly
were: General Stanley Scott, General Don Shingler, Colonel
Edward Brown, Colonel Roy Graham, Colonel Theodore Osborne, Colonel Arthur Purvis, Colonel Paul Yount and Major
Benjamin Wyatt. General Pownall, who is the Commander-
in-Chief of the British Armies in the Persian Gulf Section, was
also a house guest. On the afternoon of my arrival, General Connolly gave a tea, and invited the Apostolic Delegate, and all the
Chaplains and clergy in Tehran.

In the early morning of Sunday, May 23rd, I officiated at a
Field Mass for American troops in this area. General Connolly,
his entire staff and a large number of officers and men attended,
and afterwards I spent an hour or so meeting and talking with
them. Then I drove to the hospital and visited with the patients
until it was time to meet General Connolly and some of his
staff who were going with me to luncheon at the residence of
Archbishop Marina. The chauffeur thought he knew where the
Archbishop's house was located, but even with recourse to the
police, we were unable to find it. Finally rescued by a searching
party, we were an hour late for the luncheon—but every one
was very good-natured about it. The only real harm that came
from our tardiness was that the macaroni was spoiled. This is
not any minor matter because in Tehran there is real hunger.
General Connolly told me that the Army had not purchased anything locally, in order not to take food from the local population, and to prevent the prices from rising.

The next day I had an hour's audience with King Mohamad Riza Shah Pahlavi of Iran. His palace, built of onyx, alabaster and other precious marbles, is truly magnificent. Some rooms are paneled with wood inlaid with mother-of-pearl. The King is a young man, of average height, slender in stature. Educated in Switzerland, he was very young when he succeeded his father who was banished and now lives in exile. The King is deeply interested in his country's welfare and is anxious to get the cooperation of other governments in the tasks before him. He knows the seriousness of the problems in public health, administration, agriculture, and education.

Iran is the modern name for Persia. This name was given to the region around Persepolis, which was the capital during the time of Persia's great military ascendency. Iran takes its name from the great plateau that forms the central part of the country. In spite of naturally favorable conditions, however, many people do not have enough to eat. As inevitably follows when there is hunger, there is also much sickness and a high rate of infant mortality. Certainly, both the hunger and the high morbidity and mortality rates are remediable for the climate is good and the soil is fertile.

Tehran, like many of the other cities in the Middle East, presents pathetic and challenging contrasts of wealth and poverty, splendor and squalor. There are large government buildings, including a Palace of Justice with a thousand rooms, a modern bank building, and an impressive railroad station. In startling contrast, however, on wide tree-lined streets, is the sight of water flowing down from the hills, probably pure before it strikes the city, passing through open gutters and being used for the washing of clothes, feet, and animals, and also for drinking purposes.

While I have been turned upside down and inside out by joltings in airplanes, nothing has retched my stomach more, than seeing people cup handfuls of water out of these gutters for their babies and themselves to drink. No wonder that all manner of diseases, from dysentery to Baghdad boils, are so prevalent.

America is striving to help Iran medically and economically, and I think that Iranians welcome and appreciate our help. Dr. Millspaugh, an American economist, who knows Iran and who is respected here, has just been named Minister of Finance. I understand that this position is not only a position of honor but one of authority and power. Mr. Joseph Sheridan, another American, is Minister of Food Supplies.

There is great admiration here for the efficient manner in which the Russians are conducting the war. That admiration is expressed not only here but universally. The valiant defense of their country, the relentless pressing of the invaders from their soil, and the superb military, and national leadership the Russians have had in doing these things, merit not only praise but gratitude. For Germany's power would have been overwhelming on the western front if Germany herself had not opened up her second front on Russia.

England and America must ever acknowledge Russia's indispensable aid. On our side we have helped Russia. We are sending to Russia more planes, tanks, and motor vehicles than to any other front: "forty-five per cent of planes, forty-four per cent of tanks, and forty-one per cent of motor vehicles." It gives one a very definite sensation of cooperation actually to witness the transfer of these planes, tanks, and trucks from the American army to the Soviet army, and to see the white stars on our planes become red stars on theirs.

Russia, Great Britain, the United States and other allied powers are winning the war together. But there is a very strong impression throughout the Middle East that Russia has her own ideas about Peace and also about boundaries. Moreover, Mr. Stalin is not obliged to ask any one either inside or outside of Russia about putting his ideas into effect. As a matter of fact the United States and England are fighting a world war on many fronts, and Russia is fighting on only one front, on her own soil against an invader that attacked her. Many wish that Russia would open a second front against Japan or at least permit us the "use of bases" as the phrase goes. Whatever be the merits of this discussion we hear of no mass meetings held in Russia demanding that the Russian authorities go to war against Japan to help us with a second front. And my information is that two of the four freedoms as we understand them,—freedom of expression and freedom of religion,—do not exist in Russia.

Naturally, I like to talk with people of various opinions and classes in every country I visit. Frequently my most definite impressions about places and situations are from people that I meet by chance. I was deeply impressed by what one man in Iran told me because what he said was typical of what I had heard in other small countries.

Simply and frankly he said, "Iran has been our home for thousands of years. No nation has or can have any legitimate claim to our land. While we have conceded parts of it to others by reason of force, we have never appropriated other people's property. We have, therefore, a full right to live in our home peacefully and happily; but, unfortunately, we have rarely enjoyed peace throughout our history. Down through the centuries, we have been exposed both to encroachments from without, and unrest, treachery and dissension from within so that we are now destitute, desolate and wretched."

Despite all this he firmly believes in the future of his nation, and that Iran possesses not only the "potentiality for honesty," as one American has said, but that he is completely convinced Iran is "potentially capable of making progress in all forms of human endeavor." His whole life has been passed studying and analyzing conditions in his country which he attributed to two main causes: "lack of social justice, and poverty," saying, "the first cause is perhaps subsidiary to the second." Poverty throughout the centuries, with intervals of absolute famine, had exhausted almost all the moral and material resources of his people. "Our first need," he said, "is to get food enough on which to live. Ours is an agricultural land. If America would help us irrigate our land, we could produce food and cattle not only for our own needs, but also for sale in the world markets, and we could develop other resources and be helped to moral and material progress."

To achieve these ends, this man asserts it is not enough to have strong and able leaders, but these leaders must be fired with righteous patriotism that will inspire in others the desire of selfless service to their country.

"We, the descendants of a once great nation of the ancient world," he continued, "cry for help and aspire desperately for regeneration. We need a great and honest friend. Will the land of Washington and Lincoln be that friend? Will America support us morally and materially? Will America send us men who will have eyes, ears, and the will to support us?"

Listening, I saw and heard in him men of other small nations, who less eloquently but no less earnestly, have made the same appeal to me as an American.

On the afternoon of May 24th I said Mass in an open field at Camp Atterbury, not far from Tehran, for a large group of soldiers; and the next morning at another camp for a very large number of Polish refugees. Such occasions deeply move me. Longfellow wrote "Evangeline," which I like the best of all his poems, about Acadian exiles from the little village of Grand Pré. You will remember that you and I visited that village together seven years ago. With how much greater pathos and poignancy could Longfellow have written of the plight of the Polish people, murdered, violated, exiled, and scattered all over the globe. For the very young children I have great compassion. They are, however, mercifully too young to understand their situation. The tragedy of the old, the middle-aged, is more appalling. However, the refugees here are at least receiving food and shelter. They live in tents outside Tehran. For the occasion of my coming, these tents were decorated with religious pictures taken from the meagre possessions they had kept with them during the long, hard miles of their journey from home.

After my visit to the refugees, I had an opportunity to go with Colonel Brown and Colonel Purvis to Isfahan. There is a saying that, if one does not see Isfahan, one does not see Persia. This city is in the west central portion of Persia, a three-hour flight to the south from Tehran. The British Consul, Mr. Gault, met us at the airport and brought us to the town. Because it is normally very uncomfortable to cover distances in Persia, American visitors have been very rare, especially to this place. Isfahan is said to have one of the largest squares in the world, and I can easily believe this statement, for there is a polo ground right in the center. The bazaar in this town was one of the most interesting, as well as the cleanest, of any I have visited in any city. I watched the rug-making, the stamping of designs on cloth and inlay work in silver and gold. In Isfahan, they manufacture opium and a great many people use it. It is very easy to procure and a stick the size of a piece of sealing wax costs only fifteen cents.

The women of Isfahan have their own particular headgear. There seems to be a different headgear and a different way of wearing veils in every place. In Syria and in some other localities Moslem women cover their faces completely. In Egypt, the faces are only half covered.

In many places of the Middle East there are very few Christians and in some sections they suffer persecution. One sees a number of Christian women who have purposely made their faces ugly and repulsive by voluntary tattooing, so that they would not be molested. In many places in the Middle East one cannot be an average Christian. Every Christian must be a hero. One of these heroes whom I met, was a Chaldean priest, an alumnus of the Propaganda in Rome, some years before my time. One of the tortures he suffered was the mutilation of his ears. The average American does not, I think, sufficiently realize the ordeals, trials, and heroism of missionaries.

Now I am about to leave Iran with varied memories; memories of gracious kindnesses from many persons; memories of great palaces filled with priceless tapestries and mosaics and set in luxuriant gardens. I have the memory of the "throne of the peacock" of the Persian Shah, and his bed encrusted with precious stones. I also have the memory of great poverty and destitution; of deaths from typhus and from hunger; I have recollections of little boys who should be at school or at play, working in the bazaars or in the fields; of little girls carrying two-gallon cans of water on their heads.

With these contrasting memories, I think of Iran symbolized in her emblem by the rising sun and the lion, and I hope that the lion will be a sign of Persia's courage and that the rising sun will never set.

Alexandria, Egypt
June 9, 1943

General Sikorsky had asked me to visit the Polish troops in Iraq. To do so I left Tehran on Thursday, May 27th, to go to Kirkuk to offer a field Mass for five thousand Polish soldiers under the command of General Anders and General Tokarzewski.

The evening before my departure for Kirkuk I was with General Shingler, who has charge of all the convoys that come over the mountains from the Persian Gulf, some of them with supplies for our troops, others consisting of loaded trucks, which at some point in Iran are consigned to the Russian authorities. The work of the men who drive these trucks is extraordinary; in twenty-four hours they pass from summer to winter, through heat, cold, dust, rain, hail, to heat and dust again. The men rest every other day after twelve hours of continuous driving, and the trucks are going constantly.

I wanted to say good-bye to the household before I went to bed, but they all insisted on getting up at four o'clock in the morning to bid me farewell and General Scott, Colonel Brown, and Colonel Purvis drove with me to the airport.

Airports are intriguing places these days. The plane that took off the field just before ours was headed for Moscow; and other planes were departing for other distant places. Our plane left Tehran promptly at five o'clock, for the two and one-half hour ride over barren, unpopulated, mostly mountainous regions to

Kirkuk. The fiery furnace of Holy Scripture is located here by tradition.

We went on to the camp where I received the warmest possible welcome from the Polish officers and soldiers. Bishop Gawlina was present at the Mass and translated my remarks into Polish. I waited for a review of the troops, and then went to the officers' mess for breakfast.

I wanted to go to Mosul, which is not far from Kirkuk, and is near the ruins of the ancient city of Nineveh. But it was not possible. The plane was leaving for Ahwaz. We flew southward to the Tigris River and followed it some distance toward Baghdad. The scenery was varied, over mountains, scattered gorges, cultivated plains, and desert areas. It is fascinating to see villages that from the sky seem so near to each other, yet whose inhabitants seldom meet because they live on opposite slopes of the mountains. Flying at about ten thousand feet, we were only a few hundred feet above some of the ranges, which stretch beyond vision in every direction.

From Baghdad, with its now familiar appearance and its warm memories of my recent visit, we continued following the Tigris River for about an hour and then turned eastward to the Ahwaz airport. A truck took us to headquarters where I met the commanding officer, Colonel Pettit, and Chaplain James Murphy, of the Rochester diocese.

It was terrifically hot, and here the ration of salt tablets is eight per day. To live and work in this Persian Gulf area is an ordeal, but our men accept this and other ordeals in a soldierly spirit. To me the insect annoyance is more trying than the heat, but it is trivial to mention it because altogether I was in the Persian Gulf district only a few days. However, the sand flies and other pests did concentrate on me during that time. I was fortunate to keep fairly well, for sand flies can poison one and cause a high fever for three or four days.

On my last afternoon in Iraq, I was not feeling particularly well, so I limited myself to calls at the hospital. There were not many patients, and I had visits with them all. There was no chapel on this post nor any other place where all who wished to attend the religious services could be accommodated, so we had Mass in the field. There were many nurses present. Talking with them after Mass, I realized that if we think nursing is a great profession at home in peacetime, it is nothing less than a sublime vocation in wartime. These women are brave, self-reliant, versatile and tireless. Some nurses whom I have met caring for the sick in military hospitals are devoted to their patients with a nobility that equals the immolation of religious profession. They minister to the sick not only as individual sufferers, but, in the name of the Divine Physician and the Good Samaritan, they help to salvage stricken humanity.

After brief words with each nurse and soldier, to whom in some way I represented home, I went to visit the missionaries in town, for I was told that they were expecting me. In one mission, I found Father Merrick, a Jesuit from Somerville, Massachusetts, pastor, teacher and friend of the natives, and the personification of America's love of service for others. I welcomed the opportunity to thank him personally for his generous service to our soldiers.

The next morning I left Ahwaz for Cairo. We crossed Iran, Iraq, the Syrian desert, a corner of Saudi Arabia, Trans-Jordania and Amman its capital, the River Jordan, then Jerusalem again for the third "last time." Finally we flew down the Palestinian coast, over Suez, and back to Cairo. I am almost a commuter over the Suez area.

When we reached Cairo, we had a flurry of excitement, unusual in a way, because everyone is always most docile in complying with all formalities in clearance and arrival at airports. There was a lady passenger on our plane, a native of France, who had been living and working in Russia. She seemed a very capable, resourceful, determined person. All her papers were in order, otherwise she would not have been on the plane. Being a lady and in a hurry, she was the first one to present her papers when we arrived in Cairo. The passport examination, the customs, the military inspection, were all satisfactory. The medical formalities too, would have been over at once if she had had her yellow fever certificate. But no, she didn't have one. She had left it home. Some one "high up" had told her she didn't need it. She had had the inoculations, so she couldn't either bring yellow fever into Egypt or take it out. The medical officer was courteous, but he was very definite despite a whole gamut of pleas, threats, promises, and pleas again. There was nothing any of us could do about the matter, so, during all the barrage, the medical officer inspected our certificates. The lady was still talking when we left.

This was Friday, May 28th, according to our calendar, but dates are not so simple in Egypt. The calendars here show four different dates according to the Christian, the Greek and Russian, the Moslem, and the Jewish methods of computing the passage of time. It is no wonder that many things are a bit complicated when there is so much difference of opinion in regard to the date!

I returned to the Apostolic Delegation in Cairo which had

been a real home to me. The Delegation is very commodious and located on the east bank of the Nile. It is covered at this season with Bougainvillea, and other plants are blooming in the garden. Coming back here to stay a few days gave me an opportunity to get myself and my clothes adjusted, for I go from summer to winter, from dust to mud, from snow to rain, with the same outfit.

There were still many military installations in Egypt that I had not seen, so a visit to them was the first thing on the program. The English Chaplains wished me to see some of their units, and I had a very closely packed schedule, trying to reach every place but I did succeed in doing everything that was planned for me. Egypt, or at least that part of it within fifty miles of Cairo, has become very familiar territory to me. But though the territory is familiar, I am not reconciled and I shall never become reconciled to seeing slave labor, even though the slaves are free. There are many ways of making and keeping men slaves besides the obvious way. There is such a thing as economic slavery. I know that it is not the fault of any one person or any one group that men along the Sweetwater Canal between Cairo and Suez pull all the ships through the canal for three piastres (twelve cents) a day, straining, with hands behind their backs, to haul the boats—and this, because men are cheaper than donkeys. It is nobody's fault because it is everybody's fault.

At some time or other, in some way, at some place along history's road, the human race, individually and collectively, must get sense and courage enough to be just and fair; otherwise the human race will perish, at least, so far as "human" is concerned. Man is supposed to be a rational animal, but in peace time his group reasonings often falter and fail dismally; and thus he brings on war and becomes more and more animal. How wonderful it would be if civilized and educated peoples could really concentrate on helping uncivilized and uneducated peoples! How wonderful it would be, for example, if small horsepower engines could be substituted for the manpower in human chains, that is employed all day long in lifting buckets of water from the Nile, and dumping it into irrigation channels! It is pathetic to see blindfolded cows walking all day in a circle, pushing a waterwheel; but it is more pathetic to see men engaged in the same occupation. There is unemployment in Egypt, some of it is voluntary; but there are also a great many hardworking people, and too many of them, like the blindfolded cows, who get nowhere with their labors.

I must tell you of my visit to King Farouk of Egypt. He is twenty-three years of age, a grandson of the man who drove the Turks out of Egypt or, in modern phraseology, won Egypt for the Egyptians. He received me in the Royal Palace where Father Hughes had brought me on my arrival in Egypt to sign the King's Book. Incidentally, signing books and exchanging visiting cards must be what people over here do instead of playing golf or bridge.

The King brought me into his private office, a moderately large room on the second floor. His desk was in the extreme corner of the room, near a window from which he could look out into the great Square. One's first impression is that he is a cordial, likable man. To my surprise, he had a beard; I had never seen him pictured that way. As a matter of fact, he was so friendly that I mentioned my surprise and he laughed when I said, "That will mean new postage stamps!"

I would give the King one hundred per cent for keeping his desk in good order. On it were three richly ornamented cups for the coffee that His Majesty served to himself, Father Hughes, and me. The only other thing on the desk was a silver sign bearing the single word, "Patience." The inscription was delightfully ambiguous and generic. The sign helps to make the visitor feel more at ease, however, than the one I saw on the desk of the Bishop of Tucson, which read, "Just because I am nice to you, please do not stay all the morning."

King Farouk likes to have visitors in his country. He evidently goes to the trouble of ascertaining some facts about them because, in mentioning that he had been King of Egypt six years, he added, "two years longer than you have been Archbishop." He characterized his years as having been "hard years." The King very graciously gave me one of his photographs with a friendly inscription, which I am pleased to have as a remembrance.

After leaving the King, reflecting on Egypt's problems and the problems of many other nations the thought recurred to me that wars won on military fronts can be lost on other fronts. We must work and pray, therefore, not only for victory on all military fronts but also on the home fronts—in morals, health, education, community and labor relations. We must also win the bridgehead between life here and life hereafter. I believe that religion is that bridgehead. I believe that religion is the primary source of both earthly and heavenly peace, the only source of happiness. Therefore I am disturbed because religion is not making more progress. Many believers in religion do not practice their religion. It is either something good that they will attend to later, or something good for other people, or something that they feel on a mountain, or in a valley, or on the sea. Many do not seem to realize that religion is love of God, not passive but active love, not in theory but in practice, not only for others but also for themselves, not for tomorrow but for today. Complacency with one's religious or non-religious life is more fatal than any other complacency. I have found that soldiers, in greater proportion than civilians, lead lives inspired by religious objectives and do their best to observe God's laws. We all have considerable flak to go through to reach life's target and soldiers have more than the rest of us. There is the tendency towards fatalism. There are the effects of the separation of men from their families, and from the so-called humanizing forces of life. Only religion will supply sufficient resistance and resilience to men to give them victory, not only in war, but over the causes of war. Religion is a personal responsibility for every one. There are no deferred classifications in spiritual warfare.

I do not and cannot believe that all the people of enemy nations are bad. This thought occurs to me many times and in many places. It sparked once along a Tunisian road when I came to a grave in a German cemetery. Written in English on the cross above the grave were the words: "Here lies an unidentified English soldier. May he rest in peace."

My last days in Cairo and in the district adjoining it were busy ones. I had the Memorial Day Mass in St. Joseph's Church and I gave the sermon. I would like to tell you of a dramatic coincidence in connection with this sermon. Reviewing briefly the material and spiritual blessings which our nation has enjoyed, as an example of the spiritual blessings, I cited the countless men who have given their lives for our country, from the beginning of the nation's history to the present. To illustrate,

I read a letter written to his mother by Lieutenant Ward Fleming, of the United States Army Air Corps, on the occasion of the death of his brother, Dick, in the battle of Midway Island. Lieutenant Richard Fleming was the first Marine to receive the Congressional Medal of Honor in this war.

The letter is one I treasure, and I am glad to share it with you. It reads:

"My dear Mother:

"There is little or nothing that I can do or say to help you in your grief at this trying time. As it has been so often and so truly stated, 'we are born but to die.' Some day death will come to all of us. And when we view the vastness of eternity, it is of so little personal importance whether our time on earth be ten, twenty, thirty, or even one hundred years. The important thing is that our lives, of whatever length, be lives of honor and of faithful devotion to duty. Dick embodied these virtues to a supreme degree. With all his gentleness and fine sensibilities, Mother, he was a man of courage and of character. Truly he was one of America's finest. If his life was short, it was filled with accomplishments and success. He leaves us a great legacy in the memory of the good will, admiration, respect and friendship in which he was held by all who knew him.

"The greatest gift which a man can receive is that of a happy death; and that blessing, even in the midst of shock and shell, was given to Dick a hundredfold. He had received the Sacraments often in the past weeks and his spirit was at peace with the Lord. In his last moments, Mother, he knew and was comforted by the knowledge that he had done his duty, fulfilled his mission, and was about to give his life in the defense of his country. No man could do more. You should be very proud to have given life to such a son.

"His sacrifice will be forever cherished by the Marine Corps as a sublime example of its great and glorious traditions. He was a brave man and a good soldier. God will, I am sure, give rest to his noble soul.

"And now, Mother, you must carry on as Dick would expect you to do; and remember that one day all of us will be united in the fulfillment of our heritage.

"Your loving son . . ."

It was a stirring moment when, after the Mass, a young captain walked up to me and said: "I am Ward Fleming, Dick's brother." He had just flown in from the States in the bomber of which he is captain!

* * *

Having told you about the King of Egypt, I think you will be interested in hearing something about the Egyptian government. Many Americans do not understand the relationship between Egypt and the British Empire. Egypt is an independent sovereign state, made so by the British government in 1922, on the recommendation of Lord Allenby. Before that, Egypt was a "protectorate" of Britain and had been since the last war. The British government's prime interest in Egypt was the Suez Canal, which is a life-line vital to the Empire. Therefore, even though Egypt was given her sovereignty, the British government maintained its protective interest in the Suez Canal. It also engaged to defend Egypt against all foreign aggression or interference. Finally, it provided that, while Egypt itself would have its sovereignty,

Egyptian Sudan would be a condominium, which means that Britain and Egypt together would administer that territory—as they do today.

There are so many things to do in the Middle East, that I decided to fix the time for leaving, and then do all I could in the meantime. The first thing to do was to determine where to go.

As you know, I had not contemplated a visit to South Africa when I left New York, but several persons suggested its desirability and I was naturally pleased at the prospect. One day Mr. Kirk gave me this message from General Smuts: "Please tell Archbishop Spellman that I have heard from Mr. Churchill and other sources that he has intentions of visiting the Union. I am pleased at the news, and am looking forward to meeting and exchanging views with him."

General Smuts kindly offered to make arrangements for my journey by direct military transports, which afford frequent service between North and South Africa. Since I wished to visit a number of interesting places on the route, I preferred to go by commercial planes and to make my own travel arrangements. It is a complicated matter to visit some of the places I wished to go. I knew that my inoculations were all up-to-date; but I did need a dozen or more pages of visas, and Mr. Kirk and Mr. Casey, the British Minister of State in the Middle East, were kind enough to get them for me. I listed the places where I wished to go, and Mr. Casey provided me with visas to Eritrea, Ethiopia, Tanganyika, Uganda, Kenya, the Sudan and the Union of South Africa; and Mr. Kirk secured the visas for Portuguese East Africa and Madagascar. The visa for Madagascar was issued by the French, but this authorization was not enough, for one must also have a permit from the Fortress Commander, who is a British General. I mention these facts to you so that you will have some idea of the difficulties of travel; and therefore realize how fortunate and how appreciative I was to have been able to make this journey.

I learned that only one plane a fortnight goes to Addis Abeba in Ethiopia. After making sure of the date of its departure I planned the early part of my schedule around that date. I was especially grateful to Mr. Casey who went out of his way to help me make arrangements for my trip, and also for Father Hughes who was to accompany me.

Awaiting the day of departure, I attended the consecration of Most Reverend Peter Kamel Medawar, Auxiliary Bishop to His Beatitude Cyril IX, Maghabghad Patriarch of Antioch for the Melchite Rite. The ceremony on Sunday, June 6th, was especially interesting because it was the only one of its kind I had ever attended. At the breakfast after the consecration, Bishop Medawar professed the loyalty of the Melchites to the Holy See and paid tribute to Father Hughes, who, he said, "fulfills so delicately among us the role of representing His Holiness." The Bishop also referred to the fact that tens of thousands of his countrymen live in the United States, and that all have benefited greatly from the generous hospitality and religious liberty, throughout our country. I visited also the Coptic Patriarchate, of which the Most Reverend Mark Khouzan, Bishop of Thebes, is Apostolic Administrator. The Copts trace their faith to Saint Mark, the disciple of Saint Peter. They told me that in all Egypt there are only eighty priests for sixty-five churches and chapels, and that these priests lead a most precarious existence. I was touched at an address of welcome in which the Bishop said:

"Sometimes when you are thinking of the world tour you have made, please recall that in the land of the Pyramids you visited the descendants of the Pharaohs who became the sons of St. Mark."

In a one day's round trip flight of seven hundred miles I visited Karnak and Luxor. Only a small number of people now reside on the site of the old city of Thebes, which at one time had a population of two million. Across the Nile from the ruins of the city of the living, is the Valley of the Kings with its famous tombs. The valley is not far from the river bank but it is too far to walk there, at least in heat of one hundred and twenty degrees. The choice of transportation is wide for one may go on donkeys, camels or in dilapidated automobiles. Father Anderson and I chose an automobile which was so ramshackle that the chauffeur brought a little boy with him in the car, so that if it broke down, the lad could run back to the river for help. I tore my shoe between the running board and the mud guard but, fortunately, nothing but the shoe was torn, and this has now been patched in a satisfactory manner. I mention this trivial incident because it is going to be a problem for me to keep patched together until I return to New York.

In Heliopolis, it took me two full days to visit the ——— General Hospital, in which there are a thousand beds. But they were a consoling two days. The bravery of some of those boys, blinded, crippled, and disfigured, brave now even more than in battle, is inexpressibly sublime. Rightly are they getting every attention, every care: comfortable, bright, airy rooms and wards, everything from kitchen to bed linen spick and span. It is the least we can do, but one is gratified to see that it is being done.

I was sorry to find General Hurley in the hospital. He is

returning to the States. I had another long chat with him, and I look forward to a reunion with him at home. After the war, if all come to see me who say they wish to, and whom I shall surely be glad to see, I shall keep the door of the house in New York open all the time!

About to leave Egypt, I called on all in Cairo who had befriended me, to thank them. Then I left the city, passed the Pyramids and traveled here to Alexandria on the new road built by the British army. I drove slowly by the Red Salt Lake. I had a solitary walk along the waterfront of the beautiful city which bears the name of Alexander the Great. And now I am here writing this letter, ready to return to Cairo from which I shall leave tomorrow to complete my circle of Africa.

On board the flying boat Castor.
June 18, 1943

On Friday, June 11th, Father Hughes and I soared into the dawn from the Heliopolis airport, bound for Asmara, the capital of Eritrea. I had been busy nearly all the night, having many things to arrange before leaving Cairo. Even though it was a very early departure, there were some faithful friends to see me off, for I did not know whether I would ever return.

To make the tour around Africa that I have planned will take about two months. It is a journey unique in wartime, complicated in peace time, and almost impossible to make any time without airplane transportation. In peace time it required two or three weeks to go from Cairo to Addis Abeba, the capital of Ethiopia. Before airplanes were in use, one might spend two years or more in visiting all the places in Africa where this trip will take me! But as I write this, I ask myself, "What do we do with the time we save?" I do not know what I have done with the years—there must be several hundred of them—that I have "saved" by air travel. I do know that bringing the world closer together has not been the success that we hoped for, socially, commercially, or spiritually. I have just read that after the war there will be no place in the world that will be more than sixty hours away from any other place. This will not be an unmixed blessing unless people and nations improve in their relations with one another. It now seems that as we are brought together by better communications, we are driven apart in other ways.

Of one thing I am sure, no one would like to spend sixty hours in the airplane in which we flew that day from Cairo to Asmara. Today planes very properly are arranged to carry as many passengers as possible; and whether the passengers are comfortable or not is a minor matter. To accommodate the greatest number, the people sit facing one another in backless benches along the sides of the plane. Our plane was packed with men and cargo. Cairo, the Pyramids, and the site of ancient Memphis disappeared. We left the Nile, and were over the desert. An occasional Bedouin village, some mountains, some splotches of vegetation coaxed from the desert, some reading, some wondering about fellow-passengers, some noddings and sharp wakings-up for three and a half hours, and we were in Luxor.

There was a half-hour's stop to refuel; Father Hughes and I welcomed the relief from our cramped quarters in the plane. Again in the air, we were on our way to Port Sudan on the Red Sea. It was so hot that one could feel different wafts of heat, as if one stood before a billowing fire. The next and last stop for the day was Asmara. This country, formerly an Italian colony, is on the western coast of the Red Sea, and meets French Somaliland at the point where the Red Sea meets the Gulf of Aden. Eritrea extends all along the coast, and, geographically at least, completely closes Ethiopia from the waterfront.

The Governor of Eritrea, General Longrigg, met us at the plane and took us to his home. There we met Father Regis Barrett, of the Benedictine Fathers from Denver, Colorado; Major Martin Sullivan, of Malden, Massachusetts; and Major Welsh, of Dalton City, Illinois, who had come to invite me, in the name of their commanding officer, Colonel Bishop, to go to their camp in nearby Gura. General Longrigg and his staff were most hospitable, and had arranged for me to see various persons and places of interest in Asmara and its vicinity. The General lives in the former residence of the Duke of Aosta, the Italian Governor-General who was captured by the British forces in Ethiopia and died a prisoner. Before the war, General Longrigg was a civilian living in Palestine and this important charge was entrusted to him because of his extensive administrative experience.

At the General's home, I met some American officers who were in the newly formed G-5 section of the Army, the section concerned with the affairs of civil government in occupied enemy countries. These men, most of whom have recently entered the army from civilian life, have been especially selected and trained in America and are now undergoing field experience. Since I have explained G-5, you might reasonably ask what the other four branches represent. They are G-1, Personnel; G-2, Intelligence; G-3, Operations and Training; and G-4, Supplies.

The Italians put a great deal of money and effort into the development of Eritrea. They constructed excellent roads, built a fine modern city in Asmara, and promoted agricultural projects. Despite all they did, however, Eritrea, I was informed, is unable to support itself with its own products; and its potentialities give little reason for hope that Eritrea will be self-supporting.

I called on the Vicar Apostolic of Eritrea, Bishop Marinoni, who lives in Asmara. He is an Italian; and, while properly giving his allegiance to Italy, he is obedient to and cooperative with the English occupational authorities. He is permitted free exercise of his religious duties and of the supervisory responsibilities of his Vicariate. His work is at once tremendously increased and greatly decreased by the repatriation to Italy of a great many priests and Sisters.

Repatriation, exile, or any transfer of peoples, either as individuals or in numbers, can tear the heart. Some of those repatriated were colonists who came here with the same spirit in which our pioneers came to America, to work and to rear their little families, or their large families, by digging a livelihood from the reluctant soil, by giving drops of sweat for grains of corn. They had not wanted war with us; we had not wanted war with them, and yet war came to both. The lot of repatriated and interned missionaries is oft-times pathetic, too; these men and women who from all nations, in selfless service of the Master, have left their homelands solely to bring the story of the Gospel to those who knew not Christ, and the Gospel's charity to the needy multitude.

I told you, for example, about the unfair treatment of the old missionaries interned in Egypt, missionaries who had left Italy long before Mussolini's name was ever heard. But, I am sure you would have understood and appreciated the situation better if I had simply traced for you the life-story of any one of these missionaries, from his college and seminary years to his ordination and immolation for service to others; if I had described for you the impact of war on him, and on his little flock, bewildered and saddened by his arrest and imprisonment. The life-story of any one of these men is typical of them all! But let me now tell you two specific stories. They are two out of the thousands that could be told, the mildest in the grist of sorrow-saturated stories that I could tell.

One of these stories is about a family that was evacuated from one central European region to another. This family was moved as a unit, which makes it immeasurably less brutal than the tragedies of hundreds of thousands of families, especially Polish and Jewish families, which have been cruelly and deliberately torn apart forever. A Longfellow or a Harriet Beecher Stowe could well describe the pathos in the uprooting of this family, the bleeding rawness of the torn roots that had bound them to home and to God's acre where rest their hallowed dead. The father of this family told me that the grief he suffered in being taken from his home, was renewed and redoubled, when he watched the officers drive another family from their home, to make room for him in a strange land.

The other simple incident took place in a parlor of General Longrigg's home. A Sister of Charity of Saint Vincent de Paul called, bringing with her a little native child. The Sister told me her story and made her plea. She was to be repatriated. Three years and a half ago she had found this child and her mother emaciated and dying. The mother died; the father was unknown. The Sister took the baby, and nourished and nursed her back to life. She was a mother to the little one every day of those three and a half years. The Sister now wanted permission to take the child back with her to Italy. But, because there was no evidence that the child had anything but native blood, permission to expatriate the child was refused. The little girl clung to the hand and the dress of the Sister. Not understanding, still she understood; saying nothing, she also pleaded. The Sister said the child was delicate, and without her care would wilt and die. I promised the Sister that I would ask reconsideration, and I did; but the rule was in the book. Well did Mr. Churchill include "tears" in his trilogy with blood and sweat.

The next morning, Father Hughes and I resumed our trip, flying from Asmara to Addis Abeba. It was a rough flight, and the plane was still uncomfortable. Naturally, when there is only one plane every fortnight into the capital of any country, its arrival is an event and there was a great crowd of people to welcome us. There were Europeans, and a good representation of the natives.

A representative of Emperor Haile Selassie formally welcomed me and informed me that His Imperial Majesty would receive me at five o'clock. In the meantime, I was escorted to the home of Monsignor Kidane-Mariam, a native Bishop of Addis Abeba. The Bishop was sick in the hospital, but his Secretary said that the Bishop wished me to have his own bedroom. It was a little larger than a dollar stateroom on the old Fall River Line.

At a reception given by the native seminarians and Sisters, the Secretary of the Bishop welcomed me in Latin and the spokesman for the seminarians addressed me in Amharic. From his intonation I had the impression that he was glad I had come. After the reception we had dinner, which was also in Amharic and very good.

I left to keep my appointment with the Emperor in a car that the Bishop's Secretary had borrowed. I had already gone about half a mile down the main street of Addis Abeba when I was intercepted and told to return to the house because the Emperor was sending a car for me. The Imperial Palace is at the end of the town and of modest proportions for the residence of an emperor. At the top of the stairs leading up to the portico, I was met by the secretary, Tafara Worq, who took me at once to His Imperial Majesty. Mr. Worq remained and served as interpreter. The Emperor is reputed to understand and speak English, but he prefers to use an interpreter.

The Emperor was dressed in a military uniform but without any indications of his rank. With the exceptions of Mr. de Valera and Mr. Alfred Nakkache, the President of Lebanon, Haile Selassie had the simplest office of any of the heads of state I have yet visited. There were only a desk and three chairs in the room and the desk was piled high with papers; there was a picture of President Roosevelt with an inscription naming the Four Freedoms.

The appearance of His Imperial Majesty must be very well known to you, for his photographs have been frequently published. His face seemed to me to be a bit sad. He is very deliberate in expressing his thoughts. There is no doubt that Emperor Haile Selassie has a difficult task before him, first of all because the Abyssinians, or the Ethiopians as they prefer to be called, are not one people but several. There is great poverty and grave unemployment among them.

We talked about the missionaries in Ethiopia. The Emperor indicated that he appreciated the work which the missionaries had done in his country and that he had the intention of permitting them to return to take up their work among his people. I hope that he will do so quickly, for it would appear that the situation of the Church in Ethiopia is gravely compromised. The Italian priests and nuns were deported promptly enough in cattle trucks, but there is great delay in permitting other missionaries to take their places. Meanwhile, church property deteriorates even to ruin while thousands of Catholics are abandoned without baptism for their children and other sacraments for themselves.

The audience with the Emperor lasted about one hour. From the Palace, I went to call on the Bishop at the hospital. I thanked him for his hospitality, but did not stay long as I felt that the Bishop was suffering pain. That evening I had dinner with Judge

Charles Mathew, who is a legal representative of the British government in Addis Abeba.

The next morning, Pentecost Sunday, I said Mass in a small chapel, especially for the natives. Later I attended services as one of the congregation in the Cathedral in the town. Since it was a feast day, the ceremonies were held in the full ritual with elaborate music provided by drums and castanets. In mid-morning, I left Addis Abeba and Ethiopia, and said "good-bye" to Father Hughes, who was to remain another fortnight. Probably I shall not meet him again, and I was sorry leaving him, for we had become close friends.

Soaring aloft over Addis Abeba—which, incidentally, located eight thousand feet above sea level, is one of the world's highest capitals—we began our return to Asmara. On the journey I sat with the pilot of the plane and he pointed out to me scenes of battle. One of these was the valley in which the Duke of Aosta surrendered to the English forces resulting in the restoration of Haile Selassie to the throne of the Lion of Judah. Off in the distance we could see Lake Tana, the source of the Blue Nile. This river joins the White Nile just at Khartoum in the Anglo-Egyptian Sudan, which was to be my destination after Ethiopia and Eritrea.

On my arrival in Asmara, I was taken in an automobile some twenty-five miles into the country to a place called Adi Ugri, as the guest of Major Crawford of the British army. He told me that General Longrigg wished me to see the work that was being done at the boys' reformatory in his district and we went there together.

The reformatory is a very definite contribution to the rehabilitation of youth. The boys are all delinquents, and they are committed for indefinite periods. From the very first entrance the place gives one the impression of being a clean, up-to-date, well-organized and well-conducted institution. The director was an energetic individual, enthusiastically interested in his charges. The health and educational program, I found progressive and constructive. The British government has permitted Italian priests and brothers to remain at their posts in this institution, under the English director, and there was a manifest spirit of coopera-tion between the director and the religious. I went into class-rooms, workshops, dormitories, kitchen and saw the entire insti-tution. I talked to the boys. It was a refreshing experience, and I was glad the General had suggested that "I go to the Reforma-tory."

Late that afternoon I said "good-bye" to General Longrigg, and drove to Gura, where I was busy all the evening, meeting both soldiers and civilians employed in the Douglas Aircraft Plant. At my Mass the following morning, the congregation over-flowed the chapel. Later, at the invitation of Colonel Bishop and Father Barrett, I spoke over the loud speaker system to all the soldiers and civilians on the Post. I had two hours in which to visit the patients in the hospital before plane time, and I needed every minute. It is a fine, modern hospital, well-staffed and well-equipped.

It was a three-hour flight from Gura to Khartoum. I was met by Father Duross, Colonel Kerr, and Captain Young, aide-de-camp to Lord Huddleston, the Governor General of the Anglo-Egyptian Sudan. Captain Young, in the name of Lord Hud-dleston, graciously invited me to make my home at the Palace during my stay in Khartoum.

I sent you a wire from Khartoum to say that I was all right

because, on the day I was scheduled to land there, thirteen persons were killed at Buri village, a mile to the east of Khartoum, where a British Overseas Airways Corporation plane crashed. Since an account of this accident was published in the papers, I thought that possibly you might think I was aboard the plane. I attended the services for the victims, who were British and Polish officers.

My days at Khartoum with the Governor General and Lady Huddleston were enjoyable, and I learned from them a bit of the history of this region. Khartoum is located at the junction of the White and Blue Niles, and the confluence of colors is definitely visible in the merging waters. The word "khartoum" means trunk of an elephant. While Egypt is, as I have explained, a sovereign country, the Anglo-Egyptian Sudan is ruled by the British Governor General in consultation with the native authorities. The palace of the Governor General is three stories high, a three-sided white edifice built forty years ago on the site of the palace that was destroyed when General Gordon was killed.

Khartoum is situated on the north and south, east and west crossings of Africa. In addition to its geographic position, or because of it, Khartoum's history has been important and interesting. The Battle of Omdurman, near Khartoum, was a decisive battle between the British and the natives; and one of the soldiers serving under Lord Kitchener in this engagement was Winston Churchill.

In Khartoum, I found great comfort in conducting services for our troops, meeting the soldiers and visiting the missions. The missionaries here are the Verona Fathers, and though aliens, they are allowed to function normally and cause no one any concern. Their school is modern and has a large attendance. Their

Romanesque church with dome and bell tower is beautifully situated near the bank of the Nile. The architect of the church was one of the Verona Fathers and most of the work on the church was done by the priests and brothers. I saw them working on a mission chapel in the native quarters.

Because of the stifling heat in Khartoum, we slept on roofs or balconies. This morning I got up at four o'clock, and shortly after five Captain Young drove me out to a place called Gordon's Tree, where the flying boats moor on the River Nile. He laughingly told me the story of Gordon's Tree, which is a press agent's solution to Khartoum's tourist problem. After the visitor has seen the meeting place of the rivers, the spot where General Gordon fell, the native quarter, the site of the battlefield, and the house of the Mahdi who captured Khartoum; after he has purchased his tiger skin and an ivory souvenir, he is ready for a picnic, so an enterprising tourist manager picked out a nice shade tree, far enough away on the banks of the Nile for a day's excursion, and reverentially called it Gordon's Tree.

I am now on my way to Uganda, following the White Nile River flying southward from Khartoum over the Anglo-Egyptian Sudan.

Dar es Salaam, Tanganyika Territory
June 28, 1943

Leaving Khartoum, one goes up the Nile flying south, which sounds strange to us, as along our rivers we usually go "up" flying north. As we left the Sudan and came into the Upper Nile Province, I was struck by the incisive demarcation between the desert and the beginning of green fields, forests and jungles. In three hours we reached Malakal, the capital of the Province; it is not far from Fashoda, the scene of that historic "incident" years ago which brought France and England so near to war.

This stop, brief though it was, gave me a vignette of missionary life in that area. Monsignor Wall, of the Mill Hill Fathers, met me at the airport. He is very pallid like so many of the missionaries who have long suffered from malaria. As we walked and chatted, it was interesting to meet natives who through some process of disfigurement have produced strings of beady lumps on their foreheads and faces, in accordance with the custom of this region; their ear lobes have also been punctured and stretched.

The Mill Hill Fathers have missions in Africa; their personnel is largely Dutch and English. They take their popular name from Mill Hill, the suburb of London where Cardinal Vaughan in 1866 founded St. Joseph's Missionary College and established the Society of St. Joseph for Foreign Missions.

Much as I wanted to visit Monsignor Wall's missions, I could not wait a full week for the next plane, so when the pilot announced that the servicing was finished, I said good-bye. As the flying boat rose from the water, I could see Monsignor Wall, his priests and the natives, waving us on our way.

After the desert, the green fields refreshed my eyes. It was apparent from the air that the region is very fertile. The cultivated land looks like an old-fashioned patchwork quilt, not at all even and rectangular as are the garden areas of America, but with vari-shaped and vari-colored patches. I could see thick, verdant fields, green-clad mountains, islands cut sharply in the midst of great lakes, and little villages, with circular, thatch-roofed huts that looked like mushrooms.

We flew about eight hundred and fifty miles from Khartoum. This was an area which I wanted very much to visit, because there is incapsulated here a community of Brothers of the Sacred Heart, all Americans, who are doing extraordinary work in educating the natives. But it was not to be; no one is permitted either to embark or debark here, because the entire locality is infested with the tsetse fly. This fly is a carrier of sleeping sickness, biting infected animals and then transmitting the disease to human beings. Crocodiles are the most frequent sources of the infection. While the plane was refueling, we cruised about in a launch for half an hour without going near the shore.

In mid-afternoon, we arrived at Fort Bell on Lake Victoria. I was the only passenger to debark in Uganda; the others were to continue on to Kenya, Tanganyika, and South Africa. I was met by Bishop Michaud, of the White Fathers, and Bishop Resinck, of the Mill Hill Fathers. Since Father Hughes, the Apostolic Delegate in Cairo, is a White Father, he had made arrangements for me to be the guest of Bishop Michaud. His home is located in Rubaga, a suburb of Kampala, the principal town in Uganda.

Uganda has not been known very long to the white man. Lake Victoria was discovered in 1862 by a white man named Speke who had followed the Nile River until he arrived at the lake. For fifty years the British have administered the government of Uganda, with native chieftains exercising certain authority over their subjects. The principle province of Uganda is Buganda, which is itself a native kingdom.

In Rubaga, magnificently located on a high hill, is the Cathedral of the Vicariate. Though it is an enormous church, I saw it filled to capacity three times on the Sunday that I was there. The men and women sit on opposite sides of the church, and many of them sit on floor mats, and the children sit on benches in front.

Kampala is the largest town in Uganda; Entebbe, the capital where the English Governor lives, is about an hour's drive away. Although Entebbe is situated on the Equator, the climate is cool and very pleasant; the temperature varies only four degrees in a year.

This is an absorbing interlude in the course of my visits to the soldiers. These missionaries whom I am now visiting, are soldiers also, soldiers whose term of enlistment never ends. They are never mustered out of service because of age, sickness, or injury; their battles are continuous on all fronts, in all parts of the world. Certainly some of the most precious memories of my life center around the time spent living with missionaries, in parts of the United States, in British Columbia, in Alaska, in South America, in the Middle East, and now in all parts of Africa. Time and again I am embarrassed by their hospitality, for with all their hearts they offer the best that they have.

I am not accustomed to all the types of food that are offered me in every place; and, since my hosts are always interested to observe what I eat, how much I eat, and what I do not eat, I really have a problem, because sometimes I cannot eat what is placed before me and I do not wish to hurt any one's feelings. Before leaving New York, I anticipated food difficulties and provided myself with a supply of powdered milk and of broth tablets. I gave them all away at an early stage of the journey. Many a time I have undeservedly earned the reputation of being over-frugal in my eating, when, as a matter of fact, I was a bit hungry.

I have not yet been hungry enough to eat anything when I did not know what it was. There are in Uganda, for example, great mounds eight, ten, and fifteen feet high, which I was surprised to learn are ant hills. Bishop Michaud asked me one day whether I had ever eaten any ants. I replied, that not knowingly, had I done so. He said that ants are very good, and, they taste just like almonds. He also spoke of grasshoppers in an appreciative tone. In an unguarded moment, I asked him what they tasted like and he answered, "Shrimp." In self-defense I told him of a stew, half rabbit and half horse, that is, one rabbit and one horse. A traveler in Uganda has one advantage: his stories are always new! In one place I heard hens cackling. I used the sign language and asked a native for an egg to be cooked four minutes; instead, I received four eggs. One of the eggs may have been fresh but it was not the one that I tried.

For cordiality, for brotherly welcome, the warmth with which I was received into the community of the White Fathers in Rubaga could not be exceeded. During my stay with them I participated in every detail of their community life. And community life in Rubaga not only turns the clock but the calendar back. It rolls back the years to the time of your own boyhood. There are no electric lights. At night we brought our lanterns with us wherever we went, to church, to the refectory, to our rooms. Instead of running water in our rooms, we ran for the water. In Uganda, in the monastery of the White Fathers, and as a matter of fact everywhere I went, there was invariably a bottle of quinine pills on the table, so that everybody might take a dose daily, either for malaria, or against it.

As a visitor I naturally asked questions, but I think I answered as many as I was asked. Everyone is tremendously interested in America. In general, we are everywhere admired but we have a large order to fill if we accomplish even half of what is expected of us. It is puzzling to know why we are considered such an inexhaustible reservoir of good things, for on the world map we are not very impressive. I make this remark in general; to the missionaries it applies least of all.

Not everything American is considered good, however. The natives seem to be influenced rather by our less admirable practices than by our good qualities. I heard the story of an Arab, reputed to be a very kind man, who was seen beating his daughter. When he was asked what she had done to merit such harsh treatment, he replied that she was "dancing like an American."

To one of the questions asked of me, I gave the wrong answer. One Father asked me about the church bells which were very near my room. I answered that they did not annoy me; I was supposed to say that they were wonderful. The bells were brought from Europe and the whole community is rightfully proud of them.

The first morning in Uganda, I celebrated Mass in the Sisters' chapel. The Community that teaches in the school is made up of religious from every European nation. Over in the altar, painted around a niche which holds the crucifix is this quotation: "Thus God loved the world," that is, He loved the world enough to die to redeem it. As I knelt before the crucifix, I thought that it might also be appropriately written that thus do the Sisters love God, giving themselves completely to His service for the poor native people whom they serve so devotedly. I shall not burden you with the details of all the missions that I visited day after day, from early morning till late at night. But I must tell you of one of them, presided over by Irish-born Mother Kevin. Sisters from a dozen nations reside in the Motherhouse, together with a large number of native nuns.

At the cemetery I said a prayer at the grave of a sister of Father Daniel J. Lynch, S.J., who taught me at Fordham and is now in Boston College.

In one parish I had the unusual privilege of administering Confirmation to more than three hundred children. Many girls took the name of a saint that I had never before heard of, "Maria Kevina." I asked about it and was told that the unknown saint was Mother Kevin! She has certainly founded an empire in Africa, a little empire, but a real and wonderful empire of souls.

The natives of Uganda, both men and women, have their heads shaved or closely cropped, and they all go barefoot. On occasions when I had to speak, one of the priests would translate what I said into Luganda. This is the language of Buganda, a part of the protectorate of Uganda, which is ruled over by a king called the "Kabaka." His people are called Baganda, and the customs and the culture of the people are called Kiganda. Now you have the whole story in one paragraph!

Difficult as it is to reach Uganda, the country is well worth visiting. I enjoyed all my time there, in that fertile land of green loveliness, with its snow-capped mountains on the Equator, a land that rivals the lake region of any country: Italy, Switzerland, Ireland, Chile, or our own America. The soil about this Lake Victoria region is so very fertile that, as Bishop Michaud says, "If you stroke the land with a hoe, it smiles with the harvest." I thought it a good expression and I quoted it once, ascribing the remark to the Bishop. Some of the missionaries who are trying to teach the natives to farm, smiled and said that raising crops is not quite so easy as the phrase would indicate.

Both Entebbe and Kampala are, as I have said, on Lake Victoria, the second largest lake in the world, our own Lake Superior coming first. The area of Lake Victoria is approximately equal to that of Scotland, twenty-six thousand square miles; while the area of Lake Superior is some thirty thousand square miles.

I learned a few Luganda words of greeting, and I never knew so little language to go so far. Basic Luganda is much simpler than basic English.

Now that I have given you this general geography lesson I want to give you another little lesson. I was accompanied on several trips to the missions by Father Beckwith and Father Biddleton, both Englishmen, and both supervisors of schools. I was well impressed by the work and glad to see that some of the teachers were native Sisters and priests. This is, of course, what the Church desires, to build up a native clergy and sisterhood. Bishop Cushing expresses this idea very well in his booklet which he titled: "The Native Clergy Are the Pillars of the Church." The Bishop writes:

Only where the Church is established and large numbers of its members are being fed with the Body and Blood of Christ is a people really converted to Christianity. Who shall feed them? Hands created by God 'and destined for the Altar. Black hands, brown hands, yellow hands, white hands. Hands of native priests . . . a Native Clergy.

The foreign missionary labors against terrific odds. He is a stranger in the land. As in the situation caused by the present war, he may, without any knowledge of events, find himself torn from a devoted flock and placed in a detention camp. The native priest is a product of his own soil, one of his own people. The foreign missioner must travel great distances under most harassing conditions. He must live in climates especially un-healthy, whether in the tropics or amid the cold of the north. He must master at least one new language, oftentimes without a teacher. He must understand a new mentality and gain the good will and the confidence of the natives. He must dissuade them from their errors and instill in their hearts the knowledge, love and practice of Christian virtue. He must face the diffidence and often the hostility of native populations. The native priest, on the other hand, is accustomed to the climate. He speaks the lan-guage of the people. Since he is one of their own, they are proud of him. They listen to him with attention and respect.

So important does the Church consider the native priesthood that missionary territories are only temporary assignments until native bishops, clergy, and Sisters are prepared to assume the charge. It is, however, a hard, discouraging task to form a native priesthood; for nowhere does the Church relax the high moral and intellectual standards demanded of her priests. No greater joy can come to a missionary than to see one of his boys, one whom he has instructed, edified, and inspired, develop a voca-tion to the holy priesthood. He considers the harvest of his own life to be abundant if, through his planting of the Gospel seed, and through his nurturing, one young man dedicates his life as an apostle of Christ, a priest among his own people.

Unfortunately, only about one-eighth of the children of Uganda are in school. It is not easy to persuade some parents to send their children to school because they want them to work. I heard one story of a school being opened in a village and of the missionary's efforts to get parents to send their children there. In no time at all he filled his school with pupils, and he could not understand why other missionaries found it so hard to get children to attend their schools. He had a different view after a month, when the parents presented themselves to him and asked payment for the time that their children had spent in school!

Riding around with the two priests in an automobile on some good roads and some poor ones, visiting villages, schools, and people, was a precious experience. The priests were ten or fifteen years younger than I. They were full of enthusiasm, knowledge, and hope. They told me why there are no horses in Uganda: the flies have killed them all, the same tsetse flies that are carriers of sleeping sickness.

They showed me the wood-burning engines on the railroad from Uganda to Kenya, overworked like every other form of transportation, because of the war. In Uganda they are transporting commodities that, previous to the war, it was neither economical nor desirable to export. For example, rubber trees in Uganda were not tapped because better, cheaper, and more easily transportable rubber was obtained in the East Indies; but now these rubber trees are being "slaughter-tapped." As a result, the trees will die within a few years because so much rubber is being drained from them. If a normal amount were taken the trees would survive for many years.

The people in the native villages are devoted to the missionaries. They would swarm about Father Beckwith and Father Biddleton, expressing great joy at their coming. The priests would introduce me, and then I would say my two or three words in Luganda, which would please them or amuse them, I do not know which; at any rate they enjoyed it and so did I.

With them I went to the Leper Hospital, an institution conducted by the Mill Hill Sisters. They did not know we were coming, and were all busy at their duties as we drove into the colony. We wandered first into the chapel where there was an old priest saying his breviary, and a few natives praying. We knelt in the rear of the chapel and said our prayers. No one seemed aware of our presence. Quietly we left and made our way to a group of low-lying buildings of brick and cement, each with a porch extending the entire length of the house. We spoke to a Sister who came out of one of the buildings, and learned that she was Sister Brendan, the Superior. She said she was glad to see me because lepers like to receive visitors and few people like to visit them.

This Sister Brendan is a wonderful person. I would not know to which of the nine choirs of angels to assign her, but I am sure, to the lepers, the Sisters are all angels, as they are also their doctors, nurses, relatives and friends. They certainly see with a divine light because their heroic service is beyond natural powers. In reply to my question, Sister Brendan said that she had never seen a leper when, in Ireland, she volunteered to serve them; but she has been supremely happy in her ten years among them. With her I visited lepers in all stages of the disease.

Three were dying. I gave them a blessing and paused a moment at their bedsides. As I looked at their poor, shriveled, gnarled, gnawed bodies, I was thinking of Christ and the lepers in the Gospel story. Sister Brendan startled me, expressing the thought with which I was struggling. "What a surprise and a joy," she said, "to die and to wake up all clean!"

She told me that the lepers do not want for anything, that the government, the Church, and individuals, all want to help the lepers. Sister Brendan's motto is "Everything for the lepers."

Mass production, even of missionaries, makes us forget the worth of the individual; but, seeing these nuns at work among the lepers, reminds us that each of these lives has a fascinating story. Certainly, the individual is all-important in the eyes of God. From now on when I hear or read of a departure ceremony for missionaries, I shall have a much more vivid impression of the personal heroism that their sacrifice involves. Only God Himself can be, and God alone is, their reward.

All the lepers who were not bedridden or who were not then having medical treatment, grouped about me and I spoke to them. Father Biddleton translated what I said into Luganda. Then I added my own two words in that language, and all the patients were delighted. Leprosy brings huskiness of voice, but their voices sounded clear to my ear when they joined in song for me. Sister Peter Mary, a nun from New York, said to me, "They are singing 'God be with you on your journey.'" I hope that at the end of my life's journey I shall meet them all again.

Before leaving, I went to see the chaplain, Father McCloone. He came here in 1911 and has served the lepers long and well. An old man now, he still makes his daily rounds to see his patients. One of the lepers goes with him and carries a chair so that he may sit by the bedside of the sick. Father McCloone brought me again to his chapel. Over the altar is the inscription, "Dominus Meus et Deus Meus"—"My Lord and My God."

Bishop Michaud and one of his parishioners, the Chief Justice, accompanied me to the residence of the Kabaka, King Mutesa. The King is young, only eighteen years of age, and lives with an English tutor but also goes to college. When he is in school, it is etiquette not to recognize that he is the King. I do not know how good he is in algebra, but he is very good in conversation. The coffee was brought in as soon as we arrived, and the King and I sat on a davenport. I took the sugar tongs and asked him the usual question—did he want one or two lumps? He said "Three" so fast that I forgot to answer, "Yes, Your Highness." But I did say that when he was older, three would be too many. Quick as a flash, he said, "That's why I want three now!"

The Kabaka had on a long white garment which extended to his feet. Over it he wore a "Hickey-Freeman" jacket. His sense of humor remained in evidence throughout our conversation, yet he is fundamentally serious, and evidently determined to learn everything and do everything that will be helpful to his people, for he is devoted to their welfare. Many persons, including the Bishops and the Chief Justice, spoke of the real affection in which his subjects hold him.

On the morning of my last day in Uganda, I said Mass in the Chapel located at the place where the Uganda martyrs were baptized. One of those who attended the services was Louis, a companion of the twenty-two who were put to death for their faith in Christ fifty-seven years ago. That the blood of martyrs is the seed of the Church is indicated in Uganda, for there are now approximately three hundred missionaries, eighty of whom are native priests. There are two hundred and fifty foreign and three hundred and fifty native Sisters. Besides the mission schools, there are many dispensaries which administer care and medicine to the sick poor.

Bishop Michaud and I were invited to the Governor's Palace at Entebbe for luncheon. The Governor is Lord Dundas, formerly governor of Nassau in the Bahama Islands. He was promoted to Uganda when King Edward VIII resigned as King of England. While we were at luncheon, word came that the plane on which I was to go to Kisumu and Nairobi, in Kenya, could not get through because of bad weather. The Governor and Lady Dundas invited me to remain at Entebbe, the point of departure for Kenya, instead of returning to Kampala. I was glad to accept their invitation. They were very kind to me and Sir Charles drove me about Entebbe, which is a veritable botanical garden. There are groves of trees, incense and mango; trees with orange and golden blossoms; there was a profusion of flowers, roses, hibiscus in red and white, cannas of all hues. Viewed from Entebbe, Lake Victoria is especially beautiful. The Equator runs just between the little promontory on which the Governor's house is located and a small island out in the lake; and it was amusing to watch a hippopotamus lift its head, and waddle out of the water.

Sir Charles brought me to a point on the lake, not far from Entebbe, where there is a small commemorative monument. A plaque states that on this spot the first Catholic missionaries of Uganda landed on the 17th of February, 1879. These missionaries were Father Simon Lourdell and Brother Amans, of the Society of the White Fathers.

Early in the morning of Thursday, June 24th, I left Entebbe, and flew directly along the Equator to Kisumu, where I met Bishop Stam and the priests of the area. Although we visited missions and schools in the neighborhood, the time was too short to allow me to go to the seminary, which is reputedly very fine. The visit was long enough, however, for me to realize that Bishop Stam and his clergy are spending themselves for Christ. This was my last stop in Uganda, and I was soon on my way to Nairobi, in Kenya.

One of the provincial governors of Kenya was a fellow passenger on the plane. He pointed out tea and coffee plantations, and pyrethrum fields. The tracts planted with pyrethrum, a daisy-like flower, are immense. This plant forms the base of the best insecticide in the world. Formerly, we bought pyrethrum of an inferior quality from Japan to "appease" her. At that time the quantity produced in Kenya was limited by some agreement. Now it is unlimited, and pyrethrum is so much in demand that it has a "number-one" priority rating for transport on planes to the States.

Uganda is a protectorate with a King. Kenya is a British colony, with the exception of the coastal area and ten miles inland which the British have rented from the Sultan of Zanzibar and consider a protectorate. Thus Kenya is both colony and protectorate. While I am explaining this, I may add that where I am, as I write, Tanganyika, a former German colony, is a British-mandated territory. To the ordinary traveler like myself, the forms of administration seem to be about the same. Kenya, which takes its name from a mountain, was formerly known as the East Africa Protectorate.

When we reached the airport at Nairobi, I met Father

McCarthy, Apostolic Delegate, Bishop Heffernan of Zanzibar, Major General Knott, representing Lieutenant General Platt, in charge of the East African Command, Air Vice Marshal Kirby, Major General Hawkins, the American Consul Mr. Stanton, and four American Army officers.

Today there is a great shortage of food in Kenya because of the large number of refugees and prisoners of war who must be fed in addition to her own population; the blight on the maize and coffee crops has aggravated this difficult economic situation. Many believe that the food problem will inevitably become more acute in all the world because food-producing manpower is decreasing and demands for food are constantly increasing.

Nairobi, the capital of Kenya, is a most important city with modern buildings in which there are no vacant stores or offices. There is a hum and bustle about the place due in great measure to the fact that Nairobi is the military headquarters of the East African Command. Incidentally, this Command has won all its objectives and has finished the war as far as this area is concerned.

While I was his guest at Nairobi, Father McCarthy and I became good friends. Together we visited the missions and I was able to get a vivid idea of the work of the missionaries and their difficulties. Along the way, the roads at times were muddy and dangerous, and out of one quagmire, we were barely able to drag ourselves. The mission schools are poor in every way in a material sense but rich in the spirit of good will.

In some of the villages, I went into the huts of the natives, huts of mud and bamboo with scarcely any light, and saw children who were too weak to go to school because of hunger.

Some of these natives look rather hideous because their ear lobes have been pierced and enlarged to admit objects even bigger than a human fist.

Many of the missionaries are thin, drawn and sickly, but they would not change their manner of life for any other. I saw one young priest, Father Culleton, dying, after only two years on the missions. Knowing he was dying, he was perfectly resigned and "only regretted," he said, "to have given so short a time in service on the missions."

One morning I said Mass at the Convent of the Carmelite Sisters, all of whom are from Britain and Ireland. They showed me their beautiful convent cloister and garden and their only complaint was that canaries eat their peas and beans. This seemed to me a refreshingly minor complaint in a country where tigers and other wild beasts prowl around, and where the "kraals," or groups of huts, are completely ringed by closely planted trees for protection.

By permission of the British authorities, I visited a prisoner-of-war camp. The prisoners are allowed to work on the roads. They have black patches on the back of their grey uniforms to serve as a target for the guards in case they attempt to escape; such attempts are rare.

Lest I be repetitious, I shall not tell of visits to any more missions except to say that I called to pay my respects to an old, veteran missionary, Bishop Shanahan from Nigeria, who has resigned his vicariate and is now awaiting the call of the Master in a monastery near Nairobi.

Governor and Lady Moore very graciously entertained me at dinner, and thus afforded me the opportunity to meet members of their official family and their friends. The American Consul, Mr. Stanton, and his wife gave a tea which the Governor and Lady Moore honored by attending.

After early Mass on Saturday, June 26th, in the native Church of St. Peter Claver, filled to overflowing, I flew to Mombasa, where I met Admiral Danksworth, the Vice Admiral of the Eastern fleet, Mr. Hodge, the Provincial Commissioner and Father Lynch, pastor of the principal church in Mombasa. I had lunch with Mr. and Mrs. Hodge and Captain Green, liaison officer of the American Navy in this port. From the home of Mr. Hodge, and afterwards from the home of Admiral Danksworth, I had my first wonderful views of the Indian Ocean.

In the afternoon, I saw Kilindini (which means "deep water"), the well-protected harbor of Mombasa. In port there was a large number of "dhows," unwieldy-looking boats which, with varied cargoes, ply the Indian Ocean. Outside Mombasa, I went to the mission of Makupa, founded only a few years ago by Father Lawless. He already has a complete church and school and, what is more important, a large and well-ordered congregation. I had promised to celebrate Mass in the parish church in Mombasa at eight o'clock for American sailors, but I could not refuse Father Lawless who also wished me to say Mass in his church for his people, so I arranged to offer Mass in both places.

That evening I had dinner with the clergy of the Mombasa district. Some of them had come from long distances to see me and would have to drive all night to get back to their parishes by morning. They were all members of the Holy Ghost Congregation, a body of religious men established in various parts of the world, including Ireland, Africa and our own country. In the Archdiocese of New York, they are veritable apostles in St. Mark's parish, Harlem, where the parishioners become so attached to their priests that they never wish changes to be made in their assignments.

For me it was fascinating to hear about the lives these missionaries lead among various tribes, for they actually live the lives of their people. No pioneers in any land, nor in any endeavor, have made greater sacrifices or worked with more enthusiasm and devotion than these men in the mission fields.

In the morning darkness the Consul General of the Netherlands, a parishioner of Father Lynch, drove me out to Makupa for Mass. Rain was pouring in torrents; nevertheless the church was filled with natives. I spoke to them, and Father Lawless translated what I said into Swahili. Then back to Mombasa I went, where the congregation consisted of American bluejackets and Goans, who are Portuguese people from Goa in India. There are many settlements of Goans in East Africa, chiefly business men and clerks in the service of the British or local governments—people of the highest type, honest, industrious, law-abiding.

These two religious services marked the beginning of a long, full and exhausting day. At nine-thirty, I was already at the airport. We circled Mombasa and its ship-dotted harbor of Kilindini, and flew for an hour down the coast to Tanga, a port of Tanganyika. There was only one sunken ship visible in this harbor, and I was told that it was from the last war.

Bishop Byrne, a Holy Ghost Missioner from Hartford, Connecticut, was to administer Confirmation in Tanga on that day. Father McCarthy had told me of this date in Nairobi and I had planned my schedule accordingly, for I wished very much to see Bishop Byrne. The seat of his vicariate is Moshi, near Mount Kilimanjaro, the highest mountain in Africa, which I passed on my trip from Nairobi to Mombasa. Meeting Bishop Byrne in Tanga saved me a week's travel, but of course, deprived me of the opportunity to visit him in his own city. Evidently the Bishop had not received the telegram which I had sent him, for no one was at the airfield to meet me and Commander Pilling, of the Royal Air Force, kindly offered to drive me to the church.

I found myself present at a Confirmation ceremony, which was a very unusual experience for me, because since I have been a Bishop myself, I had never seen any other Bishops conferring the Sacrament. I remained in the rear of the church and the Bishop did not notice my presence. After the ceremony, I went into the sacristy. The Bishop was astonished to see me and the hour I spent with him and the American priests was an hour packed with questions about and messages to friends in America. They all came down to the airport, so that we could be together every possible minute before the take-off.

The next port was Dar-es-Salaam, the capital of Tanganyika. Our flight was over the Indian Ocean, along the African coast, over shoals, coral reefs and coral islands. We circled very low over Zanzibar, the island which produces ninety per cent of the world's clove supply. Zanzibar is a protected state and is governed by a Sultan. Mentioning Zanzibar reminds me, I just saw an airways advertisement which said that, after the war, it will be possible to go from New York to Zanzibar in one day. The tone of the advertisement is that this is just what the world has been waiting for to make everything just fine! But actually, any one arriving in Zanzibar today would not find even one small hotel and I do not think that the annual potential air traffic from New York to Zanzibar will require much post-war planning.

And now Dar-es-Salaam, which means "harbor of peace." I received a very warm welcome here from the Governor, Sir Wilfred Jackson, and Lady Jackson. Sir Wilfred comes from a family that for several generations has been well-known in British colonial government administration, and he himself has served in a dozen British colonies. The day I arrived was *still* Sunday, June 27th, although it already seemed days since I had left Mombasa. The Bishop of Dar-es-Salaam, Bishop Edgar, invited me to carry the Blessed Sacrament at the Corpus Christi procession and to officiate at the various Benedictions. I was very honored to have this privilege. His Excellency the Governor attended the ceremony. Everything was carried out with great decorum and fervor, especially the procession of the children. The outside altar was exquisite and before it was a carpet made entirely of flowers with religious symbols of perfect design and various appropriate colors. I wanted a colored photograph of the altar and flower carpet, but no photographer in Dar-es-Salaam has even any ordinary photographic material.

That evening Governor and Lady Jackson had the Bishop, the pastor of the parish, and Chief Justice and Lady Webb to dinner. Thus closed a long day, which had begun for me at four o'clock in the morning in Mombasa, Kenya, and ended in Dar-es-Salaam, Tanganyika. And thus ends this letter.

It is Sunday afternoon, July 4th, in Diego Suarez, Madagascar. There is only one other American in this city, a naval officer, Lieutenant George Bond of Philadelphia. I think that having each other helped both of us. We celebrated the occasion by having luncheon together as the guests of Bishop Fortineau and his community of Holy Ghost Fathers, who made us feel very welcome. They were even thoughtful enough to keep the American Flag flying over the house all day.

But before I tell you about Madagascar, I must tell you about Tanganyika. This is a mandated territory, taken from the Germans after the last war and entrusted by the League of Nations to Great Britain. On this trip, I have learned a great deal about the British Empire which means the same as the British Commonwealth of Nations. The term "Great Britain" includes England, Wales and Scotland; by "United Kingdom" is understood Great Britain and Northern Ireland. Then there are the dominions, like Canada, Australia, and the Union of South Africa, which are sovereign states exercising complete control over their own affairs, both internal and external. There is a Governor General in each dominion, who is a personal representative of the King; but he acts only on advice given to him by the dominion ministers. India is not yet a dominion, but it has been offered self-government to go into effect after the war. Then there are colonies, protectorates, protected states, condominiums, and mandates. There are even mandates held by dominions and dependencies of dominions. Boys and girls who study civics in England must have a more difficult time to learn all about forms of government in the British Empire, than do the boys and girls of America about the government of the United States.

When I visited a Sisters' school in Tanganyika I asked a few questions in geography. The children did very well except when I inquired if they knew what city is the capital of the United States; most of the children answered, "New York!"

Governor Jackson brought me through the town of Dar-es-Salaam. It is a clean, quiet, friendly place, with good public buildings, constructed during the period when Tanganyika was German East Africa. I enjoyed my stay at Government House with Sir Wilfred and Lady Jackson. Sir Wilfred's life includes experiences all over the world; quietly and modestly he told me about some of them. The title of Lady Jackson well becomes the Governor's wife.

The effect of the war on native troops was one of the matters Sir Wilfred discussed. There are a great many natives under arms and they have had experiences and responsibilities completely new to them. They have been uniformed, drilled, and fed in the same manner as European troops. They have traveled and have become accustomed to modern life in many ways. They have earned more money in the army than they can spend at home. After the war, are they going back to their villages; if they do, are they going to be contented? Nobody knows, but at least one native soldier from Tanganyika has written home describing the kind of house he wants the government to give him after the war!

Early Tuesday morning, June 29th, I went to the British Overseas Airways station at Dar-es-Salaam to take the ship,

"Cambria," for my voyage to Diego Suarez, Madagascar. This famous flying boat in 1937 made the survey and the initial trip for the Capetown-Cairo route of the Imperial Airways. There is a little plate affixed stating that she has made aeronautical history; for in June, 1937, she completed a twenty-thousand-mile survey flight of the Africa route, and in the same year, under Captain Powell, she made five survey flights across the North Atlantic. On the last of these trips, she made a record of ten hours and thirty-nine minutes between Botswood, Newfoundland, and Foynes, Ireland. The names of all flying boats of this type begin with the letter "C."

Circled with the colors of the rainbow, the reflection of the airplane was exactly parallel to us on the clouds when the sun rose. Our first stop for fuel was in ——, near the southern border of Tanganyika. Our flight had been along the shore and fairly low over the jungle, with occasional views of villages and sisal plantations. The sisal plant is not so good as hemp for making rope, but is now very much in demand because the principal sources of hemp supply are cut off by the Japanese. The sisal plant is what we used to call the "century plant" because it was supposed to blossom once every hundred years. As a matter of fact in five years a great flowering stalk sprouts up from the plant, which indicates that its life is ending and the roots should be dug up.

Two hours after our departure from ——, we stopped at a very small island, one of the Comores, called "Dzaoudzi." I learned that Monsignor Messmer, the Prefect Apostolic of Ambanja, Madagascar, had arrived that morning. I tried to see him, but he had just gone on to the island of Mayotte.

At Diego Suarez, I was met by Mr. Boitteau, the French Chief of the Region; Lieutenant Bond, of the United States Navy; General Hobday, the Fortress Commander; Captain John Morris of the English Army; and Bishop Fortineau, the Vicar Apostolic of Diego Suarez, who is now my host.

It is strange here in Madagascar to be seated at table, at times together with English Generals and French officers whom they took prisoners, and who have now become their allies. There is nothing funny about war, but there are many topsy-turvy things in war. A nation's allies and a nation's enemies can change about in a bewildering manner. Finland was a neutral country. She was attacked by Russia and then American sympathy favored Finland. Afterwards Finland became an ally of Hitler to get his "protection" against Russia. Subsequently Germany attacked Russia, and now Russia is our ally. Madagascar is a French possession which the English occupied because its government followed Vichy. Now those at the head of the government acknowledge General de Gaulle as their leader and the English have given Madagascar back to the French, with the exception of the city of Diego Suarez. Shaped like a four-leaved clover, the beautiful harbor of Diego Suarez is one of the grandest and the third largest in the world.

By an odd coincidence, on the day I arrived here, my route crossed the course of four Jesuit Fathers—Fathers McCarthy, Shea, Casey, and Connell—whose ship put in at Diego Suarez, their first stop from America. They were on their way to Basra and Baghdad to join the Faculty of the Baghdad College. Their boat was leaving the harbor as our flying boat swooped down to its landing. It was exasperating to miss them by only an hour or two, but I have had some wonderful coincidences, so I do not complain of an occasional disappointment.

During my days in Diego Suarez, I conducted religious exercises for British and French soldiers and sailors, and attended gatherings of various parish groups. In Madagascar many of the natives speak French in addition to Malgache, their native language; and at receptions I am greeted with song and speech in both languages. For years I have had few opportunities to speak French. Now all seem to enjoy the progress I make, not only from appearance to appearance but actually during the address itself and occasionally, the audience chimes in suggesting the word for which I am groping.

Lieutenant Fox of the British Navy, whom I met yesterday, is a grand person, and I hope to take a message from him to his wife, who now lives in Capetown. He was stationed in Basra for a long time and knows our American Jesuits. He spoke affectionately of them, especially of Father Merrick and Father Sheehan. Lieutenant and Mrs. Fox, knowing of Father Sheehan's difficult life, and fearing that he was not getting enough to eat, were in the habit of taking a basket of canned goods and fruit to him every week. When they discovered that Father Sheehan was giving what they brought him to poor Arabs, they reproved him. Lieutenant Fox quoted Father Sheehan as saying, "How can I eat when I know that those around me are hungry?"

Bishop Fortineau, with whom I am making my home here, is one of three priests, and the only surviving one, who came to Diego Suarez nearly fifty years ago. He was twenty-five years of age when he began his work here and is still active and directs all the affairs of his Vicariate. Stationed with the Bishop are three French and one Malgache priest.

I know that you do not wish me to become technical and tell

about the duration of the dry and rainy seasons, the precipitation, and other matters of geographical, historical, topographical or agricultural import. If you are interested you can look them up in an encyclopedia, which will be at least as accurate as either my informants or my memory. I shall say, however, that Madagascar is a very large island, as large as France, Belgium, and Holland together. It is sparsely populated and should be able to produce all the food necessary for itself and also products for export. But as a matter of fact, there is a shortage of food.

Because of malaria and other diseases, many of the people have become a bit tepid and torpid in regard to work. In order to get them to work, part of their wages must be paid in rice, the staple food of the country. This custom is followed also because even with money it is hard to get rice. If work is diminished, there is less rice; if there is less rice, then follows less work. But this form of rationing cannot continue indefinitely. Palestine has something similar in regard to poultry food, which is rationed to raisers of hens on the basis of egg sales. To receive her full quota of food, a hen must produce ninety eggs a year. If she has a smaller output, her ration is proportionately reduced, until a hen supplying under sixty eggs a year must look out for herself. She must go to the black market.

At one reception, I received a present of a live goose. We had the goose the next day for dinner. This seemed to be a practical solution of the disposition of the goose as far as I was concerned; and nobody, not even the donor, objected. In other countries such an action, if known, might cause offense, but the Malgache people are good natured and sensible. Sometimes visitors to countries are embarrassed by gifts of sacred animals, which courtesy demands they keep and feed. I know of one distinguished visitor to a country who admired a camel that was extraordinarily beautiful; then and there his host presented the camel to his guest. The rationing of transportation prevented the delivery of the gift.

One of the unusual things that an American observes in Madagascar is the "puisse-puisse" car, or rickshaw. Because of the numerous hills, usually two men operate each car, one pulling and one pushing. This type of conveyance is indispensable for the old and the sick, but to see complaisant men and women being drawn about by human beasts of burden, obviously at times just for an airing, is for me a disturbing sight. When I mentioned my distress, I was asked to answer two questions: what would the rickshaw-men do if the rickshaws were abolished, and, how would people get from place to place without rickshaws!

The heavy burdens are drawn by Malgache oxen or zebus. They are like our oxen except for big humps on their backs. For lighter burdens there are the men and the women, mostly women, who carry loads on their heads. While I saw some extraordinary feats, including women carrying large jugs of water on their heads, I believe I would give the prize to one woman who had her baby strapped on her back, a bundle of wood under her arm, and a crate with a half-dozen hens in it on her head.

Airmail service here is infrequent and a plane is leaving soon, so I bring this letter to a close.

Flying boat Corsair over Mozambique.
July 15, 1943

Tananarive, the capital of Madagascar, is a picturesque town in the central part of the island. The name means "place of a thousand men." It is a town of hills, and panoramas are vast. The atmosphere seems to be unusually clear, and the aspect of the town and its environs is pleasing. Especially beautiful are the sunsets, for not only are the heavens colored but the land also is bathed with fantastic hues, superimposed on the reddish soil.

The Cathedral of Tananarive is located on one of the hills. It is a dominating, well-constructed Gothic edifice, the front corners of which are large, solid, square towers surmounted with smaller octagonal ones. It is a fairly large church, and accommodates about eight hundred worshippers.

The Jesuit community house connected with it is a rambling "upstairs, downstairs, and in every direction" building, constructed at leisurely intervals by various architects or no architects. The Vicar Apostolic of Tananarive, Bishop Foucadier, called it a labyrinth, as he guided me through a few tunnels to show me the location of my room. Everywhere I go, I am embarrassed by the good heart manifested by all in trying to make me happy and comfortable.

Everyone asks about America and New York, and some of the things they are curious about are curious. For example, I have been asked a dozen times how many stories high is the Archbishop's house in New York. This seems to be the first criterion by which any building is appraised. Another question I am asked is how I can be away from New York for so long a period. Other people worry about my absence more than I do, for I know everything is proceeding at least as well with me away, as it would with me at home, for I have followed the advice you gave me years ago to have companions who are smarter than I am. And you added, "It will not be difficult." And it isn't.

Living in religious houses, I follow community customs. I am awakened at 4:30 A.M. in Tananarive or at 5:00 A.M. in Diego Suarez by a priest knocking on the door with the greeting of seminary days: "Benedicamus Domino!" (Let us bless the Lord!)

Bishop Foucadier is a Jesuit and has been in Tananarive exactly fifty years. Governor General St. Mart of Madagascar placed his car at my disposal, and the Bishop accompanied me on various visitations to the seminary, churches, schools, and charitable institutions. Having regard for his age, several times I tried to persuade him to allow someone else to come with me, but he was unwilling to permit this. As a result he became extremely fatigued and ill. Fortunately, however (for my peace of mind but principally, of course, for his own welfare), the Bishop had completely recovered before I left. Not only was I relieved at the Bishop's recovery, but the American Consul, Mr. Clifton Wharton of Boston, whimsically remarked that it wouldn't be a very "good-will" gesture if I had worn out the Bishop. As a matter of fact, if I had lived the hard life of this Bishop, I do not think I could have endured so long. In his late seventies, he has energy, zeal, and kindliness; spiritually and civically he is an inspiration.

It is unfortunate that many of the people who live in this beautifully situated town, with its wonderful climate, are afflicted with malaria and other diseases, including the disease of poverty. Good old Mother Earth has enough possibilities to furnish enough of everything for all people if Man will exercise his intelligence and good will in the production and distribution of world goods,—the material groundwork of peace! I have never been to a place where prices are so low. A chicken costs five francs, which is the equivalent of ten cents; but for his day's labor, a man receives only six francs, or twelve cents. Prices are low but food is scarce. Both rice and salt are rationed. Each person has an allowance of four pounds of rice a week. This is the staple food of Madagascar, but the swollen stomachs of many of the children bear tragic witness that rice alone is not enough protection against disease, and just one layer of potato sack is not enough protection against cold. War is partially responsible for these hardships and poverty, as Madagascar was blockaded for a long time.

There are numerous rice paddies in the region around Tananarive. Since these are mosquito breeders, I asked why the paddies are not treated to destroy the mosquitoes and I was told that this would destroy not only the mosquitoes but also the rice. Then I asked why the rice fields were not relocated in some other part of the island, for Madagascar is very large. The answer was that there would be no way to bring the rice to Tananarive; and, naturally, one must have rice whether or not one has malaria with it. However, even though I am not a public health officer or an agriculturist, I still think there must be some solution to the problem of making the place healthful and getting rice at the same time.

The budget for changing street signs in Tananarive must be high, for the main street has changed names three times in four years, the last change being from Boulevard Pétain to the Avenue of the Liberation. I remember well after the last war the epidemic of changes in street names, especially the name of President Wilson. At the height of his popularity, hundreds of streets were called after the President; and a surprisingly short time later the names were changed back again.

I had opportunities to meet many people in Tananarive and its surrounding villages, as I frequently officiated at religious services and I visited every charitable and educational institution. The Governor General invited thirty-eight French, British and American officials to meet me at dinner one evening, including members of the American Economic Mission, Messrs. Mallet, Piatt, and Sample.

Mr. Wharton, Mr. Mallet and I had an appointment with Colonel Fisher, Commander of the British garrison. We reached his home at the appointed time, but, apparently, the sentry had not been notified that we were coming. He challenged us and we answered. I thought the sentry, a native of Kenya, said, "Bon!" and we all proceeded. Instead, he said the only English word he knew, "Halt!" When we did not halt, he crouched to lunge at us with bayonet fixed. It was fortunate that through the darkness we saw him in time. We hurriedly retreated to the automobile and sounded telegraphically the "V for Victory" on the Klaxon until Colonel Fisher came to our rescue.

With the most pleasant memories of Tananarive and of the cordiality of its people; with a few more notions of geography and history, I soared away from Tananarive in a small French military plane which was on its way to Diego Suarez. The pilot was a fine young chap, Jean Renault. We came down once, in a meadow, to refuel the plane with gasoline which we carried with us in cans. Later we swooped down on beautiful Diego Suarez harbor, spotted with gaunt grim wrecks. Once more I was met by Captain Morris, Lieutenant Bond and the Bishop. I told them all of my visit to Tananarive, where I had met friends of each one of them. The Bishop was much interested in my visit with the Jesuit Fathers, the Canadian Brothers of the Sacred Heart, and the Franciscan Missionaries of Mary whom he had not seen in several years.

When I returned to Diego Suarez, I learned that I was to have the good fortune to go on a trip to Mauritius Island, which, as you know, is down deep in the Indian Ocean. I say "good fortune" because at the present time there is no regular plane service to Mauritius, and this plane was on a special mission. It was a great flying boat, and while the distance was approximately seven hundred miles, the trip took us nearly eight hours because of the prevailing headwinds that are constant at this time of the year. I sat with the pilot for much of the trip, and finally nearly an hour before our arrival, Mauritius began to climb out of the sea.

By nature, Mauritius is a very beautiful island with picturesque mountains rising sharply and strikingly, although none is higher than twenty-five hundred feet. The island was discovered by the Portuguese and settled by the Dutch who named it, and then abandoned it. Afterwards Mauritius was taken by the French, from whom the British captured it in 1810. French is still the language of the island and its capital, Port Louis, gives it name to the diocese. I was surprised to learn that the population of this small island is about four hundred thousand.

The Governor and Lady MacKenzie Kennedy, my hosts, invited Archbishop James Leen and his Vicar General, Monsignor Lee, to dinner the evening of my arrival. The Archbishop belongs to the Holy Ghost Order. He is a quiet, gentle character, about my age, and I was pleased to have a full day in his company. I began my day with him by offering Mass in the Cathedral where the Archbishop welcomed me and spoke briefly. Since he did not know of my arrival until we met at dinner, and since the Mass was early in the morning, I was amazed to find a reception committee, music at the Mass, altar boys, and a congregation that filled the church. Later in the morning we visited some remarkable institutions: the College of the Christian Brothers, the Convent of the Reparatrice Nuns, Loretto Academy, the Academy of the Holy Ghost Fathers, and other parishes and schools.

We had luncheon at the Archbishop's House with the clergy of neighboring places and then drove through the island, and visited the beautiful shrine of Our Lady of Peace, located on the side of a mountain. The statue of our Blessed Lady, holding the world in her hand, is of Carrara marble, and is similar to the statue that, in our country, is known as the Queen of the Missions. We made a brief pilgrimage to the tomb of a venerable Holy Ghost Missionary, Father Laval, who has the reputation of having been a saint, and to whom there is great devotion on the island.

With the combined help of the Governor, the Archbishop and the Mayor, I succeeded in going in all directions at once! The Mayor arranged a civic reception in less time than it would take to summon the fire department. I met and addressed the members of the House of Deputies, and the administrative officers and representatives of various organizations, including the St. Vincent de Paul Society. The Mayor presented me with a pair of cuff links with the coat of arms of Mauritius enamelled on them, and when I finally finished the day, the day had finished me. But it had given me a host of very happy experiences and remembrances of the charm of the people and the charm of the Island, the "Pearl of the Indian Ocean." One impressive view was from the rim of a deep crater of an extinct volcano. Its sides were covered with fir trees and its floor with grass, making it a gigantic green bowl. Beautiful is nature and interesting her phenomena in Mauritius; good and kind are the people, all of them, and I shall always remember their friendship. One of the most unforgettable persons to me was an old blind Sister in Loretto Convent, Sister Margaret Mary. When, as a girl in England, she embraced the Catholic religion, she was disowned by her family. Later, she became a nun and nearly all her life has been passed serving the poor as a missionary Sister in India. Now, at the age of ninety-three, calm, sweet and cheerful she is awaiting God's call in this convent.

I said that I was tired after this day. I also had a fever and the Governor and Lady MacKenzie Kennedy wished me to stay with them until I was better. The flight of the next day was scheduled to be over ten hours, for we were to search for survivors of a vessel that had been torpedoed. But I decided to go, principally, because I wanted to be with General William Platt, who has been one of the great generals of the war, and with whom I had become very friendly. He is in command of all the forces in East Africa, and was the Commanding General of the British Armies that saved the Sudan, and conquered Ethiopia, Eritrea, and the Italian Somaliland. We left Mauritius an hour before daybreak and it was late in the afternoon when we reached Diego Suarez. We had seen no survivors nor ships of any kind.

Once more I was back with Bishop Fortineau and again a member of this community which had received me as a brother. The Bishop told me that he was to leave at four the next morning for a fourteen-hour truck ride to cover a distance of two hundred and fifty kilometers or about one hundred and sixty-five miles. This will give you an idea of the kind of road over which he was going. The regular rising time here is five o'clock; so, naturally, I volunteered to get up an hour early to see him off, because he had met me on three arrivals here and had seen me off on two departures; but he would not permit it. I then said that I would say good-bye to him after night prayers, but he demurred, saying that after night prayers there is silence. So we said farewell, before prayers, just outside of the chapel, each to continue his own journey through the world and through life, far apart and yet—for my sake—I hope close together.

> Ships that pass in the night, and speak each other in passing,
> Only a signal shown and a distant voice in the darkness;
> So on the ocean of life we pass and speak one another,
> Only a look and a voice; then darkness again and a silence.

To me, these verses say much, but they do not say enough. I feel that the hundreds of men and women, missionaries, soldiers, and lay people whom I have met during my lifetime have left, in their passing, not darkness but light.

On Monday, July 12th, I took a plane on the regular run of the Air Force from Diego Suarez to —— in Tanganyika. This is a weekly service from Tananarive to Damascus, making other intervening stops in Nairobi, Khartoum, and Cairo. The plane circled over the galleon-shaped promontory in the harbor of Diego Suarez, and I thought, "Veloma!", which is good-bye in the Malgache language.

One of the passengers on the plane was General Seci, a French doctor whom I had previously met, a doctor who has devoted his life to the study of tropical diseases. Naturally, we talked medi-

cine, and the General told me of some of his battles in fighting
disease, from which he certainly derives great satisfaction. It will
be wonderful if and when we can concentrate on fighting crime,
disease, ignorance, and poverty, instead of fighting one another.
That would be the grandest freedom of all—freedom from war,
for then we would have all the others; but if we have all the
others, perhaps we shall have freedom from war!

General Seci told me about the bubonic plague which in olden
days was called "The Pest." Some of the great pestilences that
we read about in history were of this type. Rats are the carriers
of this disease; if a mosquito bites an infected rat and afterwards
a human being, the disease may be communicated. The bubonic
plague is no longer a fatal disease if it is diagnosed and treated in
proper time.

After arriving at —— in the plane, I was brought to the
dock where I was to take the flying boat. The road was a very
rough one but I had become accustomed to such roads; riding
on them constitutes good exercise.

When I reached the harbor of —— I was informed that the
flying boat was a day late, and that Mr. Foster, the Provincial
Commissioner, had invited me to stay with him. He lives alone
in a frame house, and I think he was nearly as pleased to have
a visitor as I was to have a host, for visitors to —— are very
few.

There are no electric lights in ——, and I am reacquiring
a certain aptitude in handling kerosene lamps of various kinds.
In fact, on this trip, I really think I have experienced all types
and manners of living used from the time of the landing of the
Pilgrims on Plymouth Rock down to the present day.

Mr. Foster invited some of the neighbors to supper and we had a pleasant evening. We had walked in the afternoon to the parish church which was formerly in charge of the Benedictine Fathers of German origin. These priests had been transferred to the interior and others had taken their places, with Father Gattang, a Holy Ghost Father from Holland, as the Superior. He knew many members of his congregation in America. My plane was not due to leave —— until two o'clock in the afternoon but Father Gattang wished me to celebrate Mass at six o'clock in the morning so that I could meet his parishioners before they went to work. It was about half a mile walk from the Provincial Commissioner's house to the church. It was still jet black night as I walked along, and there was something a bit weird in the experience. After Mass I met the congregation and had breakfast and a pleasant hour with the Fathers, talking over mission and world problems. We discussed social and economic questions that, after the war, will need a great deal of adjustment everywhere in the world, even in small places.

Everyone discusses these post-war problems, and in these countries, one of the principal concerns is in regard to the effects of the war on the natives. For the first time they have been clothed as Europeans and for the first time they have worn shoes. One man told me that the native does not want a better house than one made of clay plastered on bamboo laths, with a grass roof. He said that this type of house has been satisfactory to the native for generations, and is adequate for his uses and appropriate for the climate. The inequalities in pay, even when all pay is very small, give rise to economic problems; and from these economic problems that are difficult to solve in primitive life one realizes faintly the complexity of world economic problems. Any solution will require a great assemblage of brain power of all nations, working together with infinite good will and patience over a long period of time.

Take, for instance, Zanzibar and the rice problem. Before the war Zanzibar received its rice from Burma, thousands of miles away, instead of acquiring it from nearby Tanganyika where it was plentiful. This shows that the native workers of Burma must have been paid a great deal less than the native workers of Tanganyika, who received fifteen or sixteen shillings, or a little more than three dollars a month in our money. The conclusion reached by one economic "expert" was not that the native labor in Burma received too little pay, but that the native labor in Tanganyika received too much! If the people of Tanganyika cannot profitably sell rice to their neighbors in Zanzibar, one can realize how difficult and complicated must be world arrangements for the equitable distribution of thousands of different commodities to thousands of different communities.

But to get back to my story. On July 13th, as I was going down the wharf to take the launch for the flying boat, word came that it had been obliged to return to Dar es Salaam for repairs; so I spent the afternoon visiting in the native village and walking along the shore of —— Harbor, through groves of casuarina, baobab, and mango trees.

I made another call at the mission and Father Gattang told me more of his interesting experiences. He explained the difficulties in learning native languages, and told me that Swahili has nine different classifications of words instead of the three familiar ones of masculine, feminine and neuter. He told also of the battle against insects which are more formidable than wild beasts. European people along this coast wear high leather boots to protect them from mosquitoes. The white ants are another plague. Many houses are built on metal jacks, with cups filled with oil or poison to prevent the ants climbing these jacks and entering the house. It is the custom during the day to carry sticks with long horsehair attachments to swing to drive away the flies. I would think fly swatters might be more useful!

Yesterday, Wednesday, July 14th, I said good-bye to the missionaries, to Mr. Foster, and to ——, and boarded this flying boat Corsair for my flight to Mozambique. One of the passengers on the plane is Lady Dundas, wife of the Governor of Uganda, who is going to Johannesburg. The overnight stop was near the city of Mozambique where St. Francis Xavier passed several months awaiting favorable winds to bring him across the Indian Ocean to India, one of the great fields of his missionary labors.

Today, July 15th, is a full flying day down the coast of Mozambique over the Mozambique Channel. Submarines have been very active in this channel, the graveyard of many ships that were making the long voyage around the Cape of Good Hope. Yesterday we flew only three hundred fifty-two miles, from —— to Mozambique. This morning we flew five hundred eleven miles from Mozambique to Beira, the chief port of outlet to the sea from the Rhodesias. Southern Rhodesia is a self-governing British colony, which means that it is practically a dominion; Northern Rhodesia is a British colony without self-government but with a partially elected legislative council. Mozambique is the name of Portuguese East Africa. The stop in Beira was sufficiently long for me to pay my respects to the American Consul, Mr. Van der Vant, and to visit the Cathedral and the Cathedral school.

I am finishing this letter during the travel time required to go four hundred forty-nine miles from Beira to Lourenço Marques, the capital city of Mozambique. As I close I am made to feel welcome by a telegram that Captain Bellin, of the Corsair, has just given to me from Archbishop Teodosio de Gouveia, of Lourenço Marques: "I send my compliments and place my house at your disposal. Will meet you on your arrival."

Pretoria, South Africa
July 26, 1943

For centuries, the colony of Mozambique was governed from Goa in Portuguese India, but about two hundred years ago the central government in Lisbon began to exercise some control, chiefly over the seacoast area. I flew over this seacoast to reach the capital city of Lourenço Marques. Many coral reefs both above and below the water are visible along its alternately sandy and swampish shores. The great harbor of Lourenço Marques is the best in Southeastern Africa.

Mozambique government officials, Archbishop Teodosio de Gouveia, the American, South African, and British Consuls courteously met me at the harbor front, and the Archbishop brought me to his home where I was made very comfortable. The Archbishop and I were students together in Rome; he at the Portuguese College, and I at the American College. Later he was the Rector of the Portuguese College while I was working in the Secretariate of State. His Secretary, Father Carvalho, also a contemporary of mine in Rome, was with us on the interesting but pressing rounds of visiting missions, schools, hospitals, churches, and other institutions in Lourenço Marques.

As soon as I arrived the President of the Radio Club asked me if I would make a broadcast to America. Presuming that the initiative for this broadcast came from America, I consented, but afterwards learned that the idea originated here. The Club had never before sponsored an international broadcast that included the United States. Everything except writing it was arranged within twenty-four hours, and as usual this time had to be taken from the only hours I had at my own disposal, the hours of sleep. Heretofore whenever I have broadcast I have received at least one telegram. Since I heard from nobody after this one, I do not know whether or not the Radio Club's ambition to have a broadcast to America has yet been realized. I know that you would be interested in what I said because in it I summarized my journeyings.

I explained that for the first time in the three years that I have been Archbishop of New York, I left the Archdiocese to concern myself personally with another responsibility, the privilege of participating in ministering to the men and women in the armed services of the United States. Nine of the last twelve months I have passed almost exclusively in visiting places where our military installations are located, both in our own country and in other parts of the world.

People say that the world is small, but if they wish to visit every part of it where our American soldiers and sailors are stationed, they will find that the world is vast. My admiration for the valor of my countrymen and the value of their contribution to world service grows almost daily. Everywhere I see their works and their accomplishments. I note the process, the progress, and the effect of the transformation of the American people from a peace-loving, peaceful-living people, to a people still peace-loving, but now a fighting people; a brave, strong, righteous-minded people who believe that they are waging war for justice and freedom for themselves and for others. I am well aware that never in the long, sad, tragic history of human relations has there yet been found a lasting solution to world peace. I am also painfully aware of some of the great and terrifyingly complex problems that will face America and the world after the war; even, perhaps, before the war is finished.

I reflected too, that America has time and again declared that she wished no additional territory; and time and again she has declared in word, in act, and in fact that she wished and worked for the world's national, racial, social, and economic stability. These must be the chapter heads of any enduring charter of world order and peace, and the inspiration for the writing of the chapters must come from God. I believe that through man's prayers and through his sacrifices peace can and will come, but I know that by the sword alone it cannot and will not come.

For months I have lived with the soldiers of the flag and the soldiers of the cross, all fighting for victory and for peace, offering their lives for the welfare of the human race. This is a total war as well as a totalitarian one. All of us are invited to be soldiers of the flag and soldiers of the cross, not just in one battle but throughout all the war. No one of us may be a shirker nor fail to be both an idealist and a realist. Either God will be in the victory and in the hearts and the minds of the peacemakers, or the peace will be a mockery; the home, a shell; and all human beings, materialistic automatons, pawns and targets.

That evening before the broadcast, I saw the sun go down and the sky incarnadine. I knew that at that hour throughout the homeland, there was the fulness of daylight; I prayed that not only material light would shine in my country but that also supernatural light would illumine my land as the stars of the Southern Cross dominated the sky over the Indian Ocean.

*   *   *

Now I want to tell of a visit to a mission at Makuba, more than a hundred miles inland from Lourenço Marques, on the Incomati River. In our drive along the river road, we saw some hippopotami and many alligators. Many natives are killed by the alligators, yet the danger does not deter them from bathing or from washing clothes in the river. This region is very fertile, and, among other things, bananas, corn, beans, potatoes, and cotton grow easily and abundantly. The principal product of Mozambique is sugar. For miles at a time—ten miles at one time—we drove on a road with sugar cane ten and twelve feet high growing on both sides. Most of these sugar plantations are under English ownership.

The women are most skillful in carrying great bundles of sugar cane on their heads. One rarely meets a woman without a burden either on her head or in her arms; in addition she usually has a baby strapped on her back. Some of the children are old enough to notice things, and, since some babies are facing in the opposite direction from their mothers, it is amusing to see them jouncing and gazing around. The women do most of the work in the fields and while they work, they also carry their babies on their backs to protect the little ones against snakes.

Just before reaching Makuba, we had to cross the Incomati River. Since there is no bridge for vehicular traffic, small boats are used as ferries. We crossed on a flat barge (large enough for only one automobile), which is drawn back and forth across the river by cables pulled by men.

At Makuba we went through all the buildings. I watched the Sisters teaching homemaking, cooking, and sewing to the girls. I saw the boys engaged in learning many trades and occupations: among them, tailoring, shoemaking, flour milling, carpentry, blacksmithing, and the making of pottery, brick, and wagons. I also went into the fields where the boys were farming.

In the late afternoon we returned to Lourenço Marques and I had tea at the home of the Governor General. The American Consul and Mrs. Preston invited me to dinner. The other guests were the British Consul and Mrs. Lidger, and the South African Consul and Mrs. Scallen.

Early on Sunday morning I said Mass and preached a short sermon in the Sacred Heart Church, which is in the suburbs of Lourenço Marques. Afterwards I visited a hospital conducted by the Franciscan Missionaries of Mary, where there were American and British seamen who had been rescued from torpedoed ships. In addition to the ordinary perils of being torpedoed and shipwrecked, they suffered dangers from man-eating sharks and swordfish. They told me exciting and gruesome tales of drifting for days in lifeboats, of sharks following them, of their captain being taken prisoner by the submarine that torpedoed them. The survivor of one ship saved his life by fighting a shark with a knife, but in the battle he lost one of his legs before he was rescued.

The Americans were surprised and grateful to be cared for so well in a place so far from home. One British sailor who had never seen a Sister before and who could speak neither Portuguese nor French, asked me to be sure to tell the Sisters how grateful he was for their care.

One of the unusual persons that I met in the hospital was Sister Violet Susman, of St. John's Medical Society. For a great many years she had been stationed in Tokyo. She had been evacuated from Japan, and was on her way to England when she was taken ill and brought to this hospital. For many months she has been here, and she was so patient in her illness that the Sisters called her a saint. She asked me to see Mrs. Frank Sheed in New York and tell her about her brother, Father Ward. He had been a missionary in Japan for many years, and for eight months was confined in a Japanese prison. Father Ward was evacuated on the same boat as the Sister, but he died at sea on the way from Lourenço Marques to England.

One more place that I must describe is the beautiful new Cathedral of Lourenço Marques, finished but not yet dedicated. An original statue of St. Francis Xavier, the Apostle of the Indies, especially impressed me. It is above the altar on the Gospel side of the transept. I asked the Archbishop if it was the gift of any particular donor and when he said that it was not, I asked him to permit it to be the gift of the Archdiocese of New York to the Archdiocese of Lourenço Marques.

To get from Mozambique to South Africa I had the novelty of a train ride, leaving Lourenço Marques on Sunday afternoon, July 18th. The names of train travelers are published in the paper, and at various stations along the way people came to see me. Some of them had boys in the service, whom I had met in the Middle East. Mr. and Mrs. Sturridge Adam drove fifty miles to Nelspruit, over the South African border. Many years ago, during the first World War, I knew the family in England. They had come to the station to hear about their son whom I had met only a few months ago near Cairo.

I might have stopped in Nelspruit if I could have had the time to have visited Kruger National Park. This park, eight thousand square miles, about the size of Massachusetts, is the world's greatest zoo, the home of almost every species of animal from elephants and lions to rabbits.

On my arrival in Pretoria on Monday, July 19th, I was met at the railroad station by Bishop O'Leary, Vicar Apostolic of Transvaal, representatives of General Smuts, Honorable Lincoln MacVeagh of the American Legation, the Apostolic Delegate, and Father O'Brien of the Redemptorist Community, with whom I was to make my Pretoria home. There were others at the railroad station including representatives of the press. One lady reporter asked me if I had any statement to make and I replied that I was pleased to be in South Africa. "You wouldn't care to explain why you came to South Africa, would you?" said the lady, with a marked crescendo intonation on "why". True to my ancestry, I countered with a question, "Does anyone have to give a reason for coming to South Africa?"

General Smuts sent me a message through Mr. DuPlessis of the Department of State, inviting me to call on him at eleven o'clock. He also informed me that the General was placing his own automobile at my disposal. Wing Commander Hull, a Benedictine Father, Chaplain of the Air Force, then handed me a schedule that made be think of crowded New York days. However, at that particular moment, I did not think of much else except that I was to see General Smuts at eleven o'clock.

The capitol is a most impressive building situated far up on a hillside. Although it is a mammoth structure, I think it looks even larger than actually it is, because of the colonnades along its great façade. I reached General Smuts' office fifteen minutes before the appointed time and met the General's secretary, Mr. Cooper, who, to my surprise, at once brought me into the office of the Prime Minister.

The General is neither short nor tall, thin nor fat, but I would say that his size is the only average thing about him. His stature as patriot, statesman, soldier, and executive, in many respects touches the legendary. General Smuts seems to be many historical personages combined in one. But make no mistake, he does not belong only to past history. He is very much in the history-making of the present and the future. His march through life, long and arduous though it has been, has by no means weighted and worn him with seventy-two years; for his manner, his actions, his eyes, his speech—everything about him betokens vision and vigor.

His office is small; his desk occupies one corner of it. As I entered the room, he immediately rose from his desk and came forward to greet me. There was no "sizing up" of each other. Instantly he seemed to accept me, and instantaneously I felt warm toward him.

I did not have to meet General Smuts to know that he is one of the great men of our era. I knew that from papers and people. However, as children in school are fascinated by tracing a figure on thin paper over an image, so also there is a fascination in superimposing one's personal impressions and experiences over the pattern that reading and hearing about a person have already sketched in the mind.

Only God "searcheth all hearts." But men can have impressions of other men, and it is my impression that the chief component part of the greatness of General Smuts is integrity: I believe he says exactly what he means, no more and no less, and that he does exactly as he says he will do. I had read several biographies of the General. "Grey Steel" was the title of one, and the General's eyes are of blue-grey steel. Many things in the book are not favorable to him, and it is true that General Smuts has enemies. There are those who dislike him and those who differ from him.

By eighty votes to sixty-seven, in 1939, General Smuts and the South African Party gained the responsibility of government in place of General Herzog and the Nationalist Party. Since that time, he has had the consistent support of the majority of the voters in the Union. The issue on which General Smuts came into government was on the participation of the Dominion of the Union of South Africa in the war as one of the Allies.

General Smuts' philosophy of government is expressed by what he said when he was working to weld together the South African Union: "We must have union. Two such people as the Dutch and the English must unite or try to exterminate each other. There is only one road to salvation—the road to union." This theory of government might have an application not only to South Africa but also to the world.

Most of the conversation during the first visit that I had with Field Marshal Smuts (or, as he prefers, General Smuts) concerned the present war and world situations. But the talks I enjoyed most were those of the earlier years in South African history, for he himself is much of that history. The Union of South Africa is only thirty-three years old; and both before and after the beginnings of the Union, General Smuts has always been a participating personality and oftentimes a determining one in its life.

I heard the General describe the action in one of the battles of the Boer War, in which he had taken part; and this experience and experiences like it make history seem very vivid.

One day I had luncheon with General Smuts in the recently constructed residence of the Prime Minister of South Africa. It is a modified modernistic, two-storied, elongated building on the top of a hill. Its front faces one of the principal residential streets of

Pretoria; the rear overlooks a tremendous sweep of valley. The residence is called "Libertas."

General Smuts does not live there, for he prefers nightly to go back to the farm he loves, to the life he loves, and to the wife who has been as much of an inspiration to the South African people as her husband has been their leader. General and Mrs. Smuts are much of the South Africa of the past and of the present, and they may be much of the Africa of the future. I remember very well something an English lady told me about General and Mrs. Smuts. This lady has lived in Africa nearly all her adult life. "General Smuts is admired, respected, and feared," she said, "Mrs. Smuts is loved."

Alertness and buoyancy are dominating notes in the General's disposition. He has also another quality of which reading and hearing about him had not apprised me, and that is a sense of humor. For example, introducing me to Mr. Hofmeyr, the Vice Premier of the Union, the General said that he is Minister of Finance and also Minister of Education. I remarked that this seemed an unusual combination of office-holding. General Smuts smilingly said that he had assigned these posts to Mr. Hofmeyr so that they would be mutually restrictive.

I intended to call next on the American Minister, Lincoln MacVeagh, but, as chance would have it, I met him as I was leaving the office of General Smuts. It seemed as if every day thereafter we saw each other at dinner, in fact so many times that I asked him if he had heard an ambassador described as a man who had only one stomach to give for his country!

Unfortunately, I had only two weeks in South Africa, remaining during that time in the province of the Transvaal. I visited its two principal cities, Pretoria and Johannesburg, or "Jo'burg", as the South Africans call it. Pretoria is the seat of the government for administrative purposes; Capetown, in the Cape Province, is the legislative capital; and Bloemfontein, in the Orange Free State, is the judicial capital. I never realized how vast South Africa is until I came here. Including the mandated territory of the former German Southwest Africa, it covers 795,000 square miles, more than the combined areas of Germany, Holland, Belgium, France, Spain, Portugal and Italy.

There are two official languages in the Union, English and Afrikaans which is a variation of Dutch. Both are used in official, commercial, and social life. Street, bus, and store signs, as well as postage stamps, are all printed in these two languages.

Whatever their ancestry, whether English, Dutch, French, or German, all South Africans consider themselves only South Africans, just as we in America, whatever our ancestry, consider ourselves Americans. In all this great country of South Africa, there are approximately only eleven million people: less than three millions of "whites," who call themselves Europeans; about eight million natives; and about two hundred and fifty thousand Asiatics. I have been informed that there are so-called racial problems: one, between the British and the Boers, which name means "farmers"; another between "whites" and "blacks."

Bishop O'Leary took charge of me for a few days, and we visited institutions, missions, and other places of interest in Johannesburg. The night we arrived, there was a reception in City Hall, and the Mayor, welcoming me, said he hoped I would find that South Africa had a heart of gold above the gold in her earth. And I did find this heart of gold in all the people I met.

As you know, gold mines in South Africa are the greatest in

the world, producing more than a third of the entire supply. Since this metal was discovered near Johannesburg, in 1886, I was told that gold to the value of over fifteen hundred million pounds sterling has been taken from these mines. I gladly accepted the invitation to go down into what was described to me as the world's deepest mine, more than a mile and a half below the earth's surface. For this experience, which lasted four hours, I was obliged to put on a complete miner's outfit, from rubber boots to a steel helmet.

This "Robinson Deep" mine at the present time employs ten thousand men: nine thousand natives and one thousand whites. They work on three shifts around the clock and produce eight million pounds of ore, from which a gold bar of about seventy pounds in weight is produced. The Superintendent and the Chief Engineer took me by train and on foot through the shafts, showed me the veins with the ore, and explained the process of mining, the safety devices, and all the other features connected with gold mining. I saw much of the debris that had been caused by an earthquake on the preceding day. Fortunately, there had been no casualties.

South Africa is not only the greatest gold-producing but also the foremost diamond-yielding country in the world. In 1867, a child found what seemed to be a bright pebble, and thus began the city of Kimberley, the chief source of the world's diamond supply. I was told that the value of the diamonds produced in South Africa has amounted to four hundred million pounds sterling, or over a billion and a half dollars.

The next morning I visited missions, some of which are in charge of American Paulist and Oblate priests and American Sisters. Later, with Wing Commander Hull and Dr. Lepkowski, the Polish Consul, I went to a large military hospital. The patients were South African, British, Polish and French soldiers.

Another interesting place I visited was the Veterinary Institute at Onderstepoort. Dr. De Kock, the Assistant Director, accompanied me. He was literally brimming over with so much information that I could not remember half that he told me. He gave me many examples to show how much medical science is indebted to knowledge obtained from studies of animal life. Dr. De Kock visited America some years ago; and he told me, among other things, that in America tuberculosis in cattle has been practically eliminated. The result is that the lives of countless thousands of our children have been saved.

Dr. De Kock volunteered the information that his great institution functions at a net cost to the government of only eighty thousand dollars a year, while the saving in human lives by the elimination of different diseases is incalculable. He is an internationalist in this sense: he appreciates the contributions that men of all nations and races have made and desire to make to the sum of human knowledge, thus helping to bring the great human family together.

On Sunday morning, July 25th, I said Mass at the Cathedral in Johannesburg, preached a sermon, and visited two more missions. I then returned to Pretoria and had dinner with Mr. Moulaert, the Belgian Consul, and Father O'Brien, my host in Pretoria.

Today I had my farewell audience with General Smuts. In saying good-bye, he accompanied me to the corridor, and told me he hoped to see me in America. Placing his hand on my shoulder, he said to the group of officers waiting for me, "Take good care of my Archbishop." It was a kind and friendly gesture and a lasting remembrance of General Jan Christian Smuts.

This evening, my last in South Africa, two hundred officers of the South African army, including Burger Commander, Lieutenant General Brink, Adjutant General Beyers and Air Vice Marshal Frew bade me "God speed" at a dinner at the town hall. South Africa and America are far apart, yet tonight they seem very near.

When I telephoned you last night, I had just come from LaGuardia Airport, after completing what I was told was the fastest trip ever made from Pretoria to New York.

On Tuesday morning, July 27th, I offered Mass in the Church of the Oblate Fathers in Pretoria, for the honored dead of the South African army. Representatives of the South African Government, nearly all the members of the diplomatic corps, and officers and men of the military forces of the Union of South Africa attended the service and filled the Church.

It was my farewell to South Africa and I was sad to take my leave, for I had been warmly received by every individual and every group that I had met since I arrived; and I was grieved and disappointed because I could not go to other places in the Union I had planned to visit. When the Church service was over, I said good-bye to hundreds of people individually. They made me feel not only that I was going home but that I was leaving home.

After six months' absence, I was starting back. When I left, I thought I might be away for about three months; instead, nearly a half year had gone by, and still I had not been able to visit India and China as I had desired and intended to do. I could, of course, have carried out my original intentions and covered the territory in three months, but spending a longer time in fewer places was more satisfying. I preferred to take days to visit military hospitals instead of hours. To go from bed to bed and have a few words with each patient takes time, but for me there is no better way to spend it. The consolations that I received from these experiences are unutterable.

These boys who have given so much still have something to give, and that "something" is spirit. Here in hospitals they are no longer regimented; they are individuals, and most inspiring individuals. While I could not know each boy personally, I realized that I wanted to know each one. A man is more than a name and a number. Man is composed of body and soul; and the life of every man, any man, regimented or non-regimented, is important to me.

Of what little importance the individual is to some people was brought home to me one day when I asked a man why some of the white people in Africa do not seem to like the missionaries. He said: "Because the priests teach the natives that in God's sight all men are created equal and that every man has an immortal soul to save." If I were looking for a reason for being disliked, I would not want a more glorious one.

These prolonged visits made it impossible to go to China and India. I so notified Generalissimo Chiang Kai-shek and the British authorities. I thanked them for the invitations and their courtesies, and expressed the hope that sometime I would be able to fulfill my desire to visit these countries.

The plane of General Smuts was going north on a mission and I was given the fortunate opportunity to be a passenger. I accepted this extraordinary courtesy. Mr. MacVeagh, our capable, personable and kind Minister, as well as Mr. DuPlessis, the personal representative of General Smuts, accompanied me to the airport.

I had met the pilot of the plane, Major Herman Beyers, in Khartoum, where we had spent an evening together. It was pleasant seeing him again and I told him Africa was getting to be like New York in meeting people one has met before. Lieutenant Pinar, a well-known rugby player, was the co-pilot.

At three o'clock in the afternoon of July 27th, I began my journey home. We flew over the Transvaal, alternately mountainous and fertile, and crossed over a corner of deserted and desertlike Bechuanaland, and then on over Southern Rhodesia. At Bulawayo in Southern Rhodesia is the tomb of Cecil Rhodes, in a site selected by himself amid the rugged grandeur of the Matopo Hills. Rhodes called the place "world's view"; but, grand as it is, and interesting as must be the great range of forests and fields in which it is situated, where wild animals roam at large, I was content with the "world's view" that I had from the airplane.

We reached the Zambezi river boundary between Northern and Southern Rhodesia. Through the kind intervention of General Smuts, we were permitted to fly over Victoria Falls, which form part of the river. Major Beyers said that this was the first time permission had been given for a flight over the Falls since the start of the war. Twice we circled the Falls at banks sufficiently steep to permit impressive, fantastic, and fascinating views of this "Colossus of Tumbling Waters."

I have read that civilization is a series of victories over nature and that the diversion of the waters of Niagara for the purpose of generating electric power is one of these victories. Civilization has had no victories over Victoria Falls. Personally, I am more interested in civilization having a few victories over human nature. One American has described Victoria Falls as the "Taj Mahal" of nature. Major Beyers told me about another American who was so impressed with his view of Victoria Falls that he wired home, "Sell Niagara." The Victoria Falls are twice as broad and two and a half times as deep as Niagara, for the Zambezi River, where the Falls are formed, is over one and a quarter miles wide and it plunges into a chasm four hundred feet in depth. However, I do not think that Niagara needs to worry about competition for a few hundred years because millions of people can get to Niagara in a few hours, while to get to Victoria Falls from any place requires a minimum of two or three days.

We landed at the airport in Livingstone, formerly the capital of Northern Rhodesia; the Victoria Falls Hotel, where we stopped, is in Southern Rhodesia. Livingstone, as you know, bears the name of the famous explorer immortalized not only by his own achievements but also by being discovered and involuntarily "rescued" by Mr. Stanley.

We were met at the airport by Captain Willys, the Commander of the Garrison, who told us that he had learned just in time of the permission granted to us to fly over the Falls. "This was fortunate," he said, smiling, "for otherwise our anti-aircraft apparatus would have had a little target practice." We were pleased that we were able to smile back at him! We had flown so low over the Falls that he could have reached us with a baseball.

We all had dinner together, and then Captain Willys arranged for Monsignor Vincent J. Flynn, of Livingstone, in Northern Rhodesia, to come to Victoria Falls, in Southern Rhodesia, to have a visit with me. This sounds like a simple matter, but, without Captain Willys, it was just one of those things that could not be done, for border control at night is very severe.

Monsignor Flynn is Prefect Apostolic of the district and a member of the Capuchin Order. He kindly arranged for me to offer Mass on Thursday, July 28th, in the mission church in Livingstone. This, as you know, was the anniversary of Mother's death, so the Mass was for her. Afterwards I met the Sisters who teach in the school and had breakfast with the Capuchin Fathers.

We were in the air once more just at dawn. Over the Falls we circled again for ten minutes, or time enough for four million tons of water to rush over the brink. The spray rose two or three thousand feet above us, and a dozen rainbows played hide-and-seek. The natives call Victoria Falls "Mosi-oa-Tunya,"—"Thunder-sounding Smoke." It was Livingstone who, coming upon the Falls in 1855, gave them the name Victoria.

The hours I spent flying over Rhodesia and the Belgian Congo were passed in great part in conversation with Major Beyers. He is well informed on many subjects, including his own Africa, and I enjoyed learning from him. He told me that mining engineers believe that there is enough copper within fifty feet of the earth's surface in Northern Rhodesia to take care of the world's needs for hundreds of years; but it is so inaccessible that the district is known as "the edge of the beyond," and it is very sparsely populated.

On this 28th of July, I flew all day long. The first lap was from Livingstone to Lusaka, which is the capital of Northern Rhodesia. While the plane was fueling, I went up to the mission and had a short visit with the priests, who took me to see the school. The Sisters and the children, and I think also the missionaries, looked at me as surprised as young American children would be if Santa Claus walked into their school.

The next stop was Elisabethville, two hundred and sixty-five miles away, a modern city on the borderline of the Belgian Congo. At the plane, I was given telegrams of welcome from Bishop

Dellepiane and Governor General Ryckmans. Bishop de Hemp-tinne, the Vicar Apostolic of Katanga, met me at the airport, and brought me through the town and to the native settlement. Here I found the most complete provision for the welfare of natives that I had seen anywhere: a hospital, a school, a church, a cinema, and even a stadium. We also visited the Cathedral, a church that would be an architectural adornment in any community of the United States. There was a note of happiness in the Bishop's voice when he told me that church attendance is good and that family life is integral and wholesome.

From Elisabethville to Leopoldville, the capital of the Congo, we had a flight of nine hundred and seventy miles over the Belgian Congo and a corner of Angola (Portuguese West Africa) to the Congo River. I had only two hours, but I tried to use the time well. Bishop Dellepiane, the Delegate, is a Belgian, and he had invited many people to the Apostolic Delegation so that I could have the pleasure of meeting them. General Ryckmans, also, had some friends at his home, among whom were Bishop Six, Vicar Apostolic of Leopoldville, and the American Consul, Mr. Mallon, and his wife. Then there was a visit to the Cathedral and a school, and a ride about the city.

I learned at Leopoldville that General Marchand, the Commanding General of the French Forces, had invited me to be a passenger in a plane of the Fighting French, which was leaving Brazzaville on the following morning to fly to Accra on the Gold Coast. Brazzaville, the capital of French Equatorial Africa, is just across the Congo River from Leopoldville. There are two launches that do this ferry service and they leave opposite points on the river at the same time. This schedule is adopted so that, in case one of the boats becomes disabled, the other one may try to rescue the passengers in the disabled boat. It is just twenty minutes' floating time from the crossing point to the Falls and death.

Governor General Eboué, of French Equatorial Africa, formerly a governor of French Guiana, graciously arranged for me to be his guest. Besides the Governor General and Madame Eboué, General Marchand, Consul Laurence Taylor, and Father Leduc were present at dinner. Bishop Biechy, Vicar Apostolic of Brazzaville, was on a long visitation to the remote parts of his Vicariate. I said good-bye to the Governor General and his wife that evening because the next morning, an hour before daybreak, Father Leduc came to the house to bring me to the mission for Mass. I brought my bags with me and went from the church to the airport. Vice Consul and Mrs. Mann, and Major Kenyon Bolton, of the United States Army, son of Congresswoman Bolton, were at the field.

While we were waiting to take off, I was surprised to see coming over the river from the Belgian Congo, a Lockheed plane with familiar South African markings. Major Beyers and the crew had flown over to say good-bye again. It was the first time I have been "seen off" by a plane.

We first flew to Pointe Noire, on the Atlantic Ocean, and then up the coast of French Equatorial Africa. I had not seen the Atlantic since my flight from Britain to Africa. With the map, I noted the few towns in the long stretches of jungle. The names were all new to me. A little more than half way on the journey to Libreville, we passed a place called Olindé, which is near the mouth of the Okano River. The plane was flying low and the scenery was superb, reminding me of the Chilean and Italian Lakes or the Thousand Islands in the St. Lawrence River.

At Libreville we had a two-hour stop. Monsignor Tardy, Vicar

Apostolic of Gabon, was on a visitation, but I went with Father Jean Baptiste Fauret, to visit the Seminary. Father Fauret told me that Monsignor Tardy would be away five months visiting different stations by boat, cart, donkey, and on foot. At the Seminary, I spoke to the native boys who are studying there. Once more I had the experience of seeing men, zealous and patiently persevering, striving to make the Christ they serve better known and better loved by others.

From Libreville we flew across the Gulf of Guinea for nine hundred and forty miles to Accra. Here I was met by General Earl Hoag, Major Scott, and Father Rigney who told me of the death of Father Regis Barrett in Eritrea, about whom I wrote to you six weeks ago and who was then in perfect health. Death makes no appointments.

I was informed that there was a plane leaving for the States at two o'clock in the morning. This was good news as it would give me an opportunity to see and talk with the soldiers in Accra. Father Rigney brought me on a courtesy call to the Governor of the Gold Coast, Sir Alan Burns. I had the opportunity of speaking publicly to several thousand soldiers but I could not meet them personally because neither they nor I had the time; they had to go to the movies and I had to go to America.

The next morning, Saturday, July 30th, we stopped at Ascension Island in the Atlantic Ocean, where the Chaplain, Father Anthony J. Urbanski of the Diocese of Omaha, arranged for me to say Mass in the Post Library. I met Colonel Mullenix and a number of officers and men, and in two hours I was on my way to Natal in Brazil.

There is quite a contrast between the peaceful atmosphere of the city of Natal and the bustle of Natal's airport, ———. This airport is larger than LaGuardia field, and it is many times as busy as LaGuardia was even before the war. I had never heard its name; and one would not immediately think of its importance in connection with our successful North African campaigns. Nevertheless, it was definitely an essential factor in General Montgomery's epic advance through the western desert, for through ——— they moved planes and supplies of every kind.

I had a part of the afternoon and the evening in Natal, so I went to the town to call on the Bishop. I had supper with General Stratemeyer, Colonel Wheeler, and Father Harrison Martin of the Archdiocese of New Orleans.

At two o'clock in the morning of July 31st I left Natal for Belem where I arrived about eight o'clock. Father Ryan and Father Lasota arranged for me to say Mass during my two-hour stop here and at ten o'clock I was on my way to ——— in British Guiana where I arrived in mid-afternoon. A short stop here, a visit to the cemetery, and once more in the air, flying over the Caribbean. We arrived in Puerto Rico at ten o'clock at night. An hour's stop was far too short a time for Puerto Rico, but I had been there before and sometime I may get back again.

An hour later we left Puerto Rico for Miami. By this time, all of us in the plane had become very well acquainted. Some of the passengers were wounded soldiers. One had been wounded in an airplane in flight over the sea, for German submarines are now armed and sometimes, instead of submerging, they remain on the surface and shoot at the airplanes. One of the passengers was an airplane manufacturer, who was not so optimistic as some people about flying ourselves into prosperity after the war even though we can now produce twenty times as many planes in a month as there were in service in the whole country before the war.

At four o'clock on the morning of August 1st the great moment came. We bounced down to the ground at the Miami airport and, spontaneously, all cheered.

I had time to go to the Jesuit Church in Miami with Father Thomas J. Hay, and Father Joseph T. Maring, S.J., attached to the Church of the Gesu in Miami, to celebrate Mass. This was the fifth Mass I had offered in five different countries on five successive mornings.

Early on Sunday morning I left Miami, and from the Washington airport, I telephoned to New York that I was home. The same three friends who saw me off, Bishop O'Hara, Bishop McIntyre, and Monsignor Casey, met me at LaGuardia Field; and with them was Father Shea.

After I telephoned to you, Bishop McIntyre made it public that I was back in New York. I understand that exactly at the time of my arrival at the airport, a radio commentator stated that as he was speaking, the Archbishop of New York was in the Vatican, conferring about something or another.

In the twenty-four weeks that I have been away from New York, I have traveled approximately 46,000 miles and visited countries in Europe, Asia, Africa, and South America. As I look back over the weeks, I would say that my visit to the Holy Father was for me the happiest and saddest experience of my journey. I was happy to receive the blessing of the Holy Father and have the inspiration of witnessing again his sanctity of life and his high purposes and efforts for humanity's salvation. I was saddened in the vision of the weight of the cross he carries. His Holiness painfully and poignantly bears and feels the sorrows of all the world, human sorrows and national sorrows. Unceasingly does he labor and pray for peace with justice for all mankind, for all nations, for all peoples.

It was one of the greatest experiences of my life to see with my own eyes the tremendous entity of America's war effort, the loyal, determined spirit and contribution of all men and women in our armed services, the quality and quantity of supplies produced and delivered by our men and women in industry and in agriculture. It was most reassuring to see evidences of the close collaboration of our countrymen with the forces and the efforts of our allies. This cooperation is something that is heartening not alone for victory but also for peace.

During long hours in the airplane on my five-day journey of 11,455 miles from South Africa to New York, I pondered over the multitude of impressions which I have in my mind and heart.

From close contacts with men of our armed forces, I am convinced that our soldiers are doing more for us than defending our land, our lives and our ideals. They are inspiring us to a renewal of faith in our country. Like Crusaders of old, they have gone into battle for the country they love, and for the cause in which they believe.

Living with our soldiers has inspired me to write an American creed with which I close this letter to you:

I believe in America:
In her high destiny under God to stand before the people of the earth as a shining example of unselfish devotion to the ideals

that have, under God, made us a great nation; the Christian ideal of liberty in harmonious unity, builded of respect for God's image in man and every man's right to life, liberty and happiness.

I believe in America:

For the blood in the veins of America, our heart's blood comes from the wounds of many peoples, chaliced in humanity's name upon the altar of liberty.

I believe in America:

Not because of the tremendous resources of her fields and mountains, rivers and lakes, valleys and plains, but rather because America has been and must ever continue to be, under God, the Beacon of Liberty, the Hope of the Oppressed, the Refuge of the Weak, the Pledge and the Proof that humanity can live in mutual respect based on the law of God, voiced through the conscience of man, and in mutual esteem, based on the responsibility of democratic life.

Lastly, I believe in America:

Because I believe in God and God's Providence that has been over us from the earliest days of our beginnings. Believing in God, I am confident both of His merciful forgiveness of our national sins and His awareness of our national virtues. Believing in God's Providence, I am confident of our high resolve that this fair land, the visible setting of the vast, immaterial soul of the American nation, shall never lose its initial consecration to the common Fatherhood of God, so that we and our children's children shall live in peace and harmony among ourselves and with our neighbors. In this America, I believe; for this America, I live; for this America, I and millions of others stand ready to die.

Index

Index

245